MY FATHER WAS A BRUSH COMPANY REPRESENTATIVE

Volume 1

(Mostly True)

LEON BROOME

'Never let the truth stand in the way of a good story...'
(Mark Twain)

I apologise unreservedly to anyone I may have misrepresented, maligned, misquoted or simply lied about in the pages that follow.

For Joseph Diggory Broome and Charlie Gabriel Broome.

CONTENTS

CHAPTER 1   A CHIP OFF THE OLD BLOCK

CHAPTER 2   LIKE THE COMPACT FAMILY HATCHBACK

CHAPTER 3   THE POWER OF HOODOO

CHAPTER 4   WORLD REFUGEE YEAR & THE GUN

POWDER PLOT

CHAPTER 5   THE MUNTS, THE CHICKS, THE NIBLETTS &

THE GIBLETTS

CHAPTER 6   HANDS OFF BERROW

CHAPTER 7   VERY QUIET FOR A JEW

CHAPTER 8   SEXEY BEAST

CHAPTER 9   HAND SHANDIES & HAND-ME-DOWNS

CHAPTER 10   CLEAN ROUND THE BEND

CHAPTER 11   FIRST LOVE

CHAPTER 12   THE OH BE JOYFULS

CHAPTER 13   BREAKING UP IS *BIT EASY* TO DO

CHAPTER 14   ALL EYES ON ME

CHAPTER 15   POETRY 'N' MOTION

CHAPTER 16   THE L IN LONDON

CHAPTER 1

A CHIP OFF THE OLD BLOCK

'It's OK. They've banned the bomb.' That was a lie. 'And they've castrated Jimmy Savile.' That was also a lie, though a little spooky given what happened to the track suited, bleached blonde Sir Fix It a few years later. But it was what the silly old bugger would have wanted to hear on his deathbed. And who was I to deny him that? His two greatest wishes come true.

Well, just in case you're wondering, I was his son.

Not always a very good son, but then he was not always a very good father and, to quote the man himself, 'Do as you would be done by'.

But I'm getting ahead of myself. Long before I stood by his hospital bed looking down at him and telling him those two little white lies, Gordon Henry Broome, my dad, had been much more than just a chalk white shell of his former self.

In no particular order, he'd been the boy nicknamed Eugene because of his impossibly and permanently wavy hair. He'd been a teenage runaway and, for six pence a night, a guest at London's Rowton House, the 'working man's hotel' established by philanthropist, Montagu Cory. He'd been a harbinger of hellfire and brimstone on Speakers Corner and a student at the Slade School of Fine Art. He'd been a kitchen porter, a conscientious objector and a timber feller. He'd been the suitor my mother's mother hoped and prayed would never darken her doorstep again and the food reformist who whisked his young wife off to a vegetarian commune only to discover their fellow residents were interested in swapping much more than just recipes. He'd been a window dresser at one of Birmingham's more fashionable department stores and a night watchman at Pontins - Fred Pontin's attempt to out-camp Billy Butlin. He'd marched on Aldermarston waving a placard demanding nuclear disarmament. He'd been the *Man From The Pru* and the Mr. Fixit who came to repair your typewriter.

Selling bacon butties, hot dogs and teas from a brightly painted caravan parked on the sands between Brean Down and the village of Berrow in Somerset where we lived, he'd fed and watered sun-burned holidaymakers down from Brum.

And, travelling the length and breadth of the country, he'd sold just about everything, from the smell of fresh baked bread to toilet rolls, bird seed, cheddar cheese, household goods and herbal remedies for family pets.

He'd done stuff, my dad.

Everyone said he was *a bit of a character* and he revelled in his reputation.

He grew a goatee. He drew crowds sculpting naked women out of wet sand on the beach at Burnham-on-Sea., the holiday resort just up the road from Berrow. He made Plaster of Paris busts of George Bernard Shaw and Winston Churchill.

He wore a Harris Tweed deerstalker, a roll neck jumper and corduroy trousers. He glazed his lazy left eye with a monocle. And when he wasn't puffing on a De Reske filter tip that dangled nonchalantly from a tortoiseshell cigarette holder, he smoked a meerschaum pipe.

He dabbled in antiques - a *Lovejoy* before his time in the West Country auction rooms of Palmer & Snell. He bought a grand piano, threw back his head and belted out *Danny Boy* till the rafters of our tumbled down cottage shook. He bought a mouth organ and became a low-rent, high plains drifter playing *Streets of Laredo* by the flickering light of the campfires that in the summer months lit up the local dunes.

He cultivated interesting and eccentric friends. Like Red Nutt, a man whose hair and temperament were both as fiery as his name suggests. And Old Smithy, who'd turn up unannounced on our doorstep riding a penny farthing bicycle. Then there was Rene (short for Irene? Maureen? Doreen?). She had a melodious Welsh accent and seemed constantly flustered. In a previous life she'd had something to do with Lord Lucan or maybe it was Lord Kagan - a peer of the realm anyway - but now lived in a half-built house on the Somerset Levels with Bill, her handyman husband, who had a glass eye and suffered badly with his nerves so rarely left the sanctuary of his fireside chair (hence the half-built house).

There was the Reverend Trill, a blind vicar who lived in a caravan in our back garden and apparently poisoned our goats - Topsy and Turvy - by feeding them cheese. There was Doug Beer, a lugubrious Brummie who ran a greasy spoon on Burnham's sea front and who I remember nodding patiently and occasionally raising his eyebrows as dad went on and on about man's inhumanity to man and the price of a packet of fags. There was Vincent Papalayo, an Italian ex-prisoner of war who'd stayed on after VE Day and somehow ended up building a rockery in our garden.

And there was someone I remember only as Mr. Periwinkle. He had a pencil moustache, rode a scooter and sent me to bed one night in an uncontrollable fit of giggles with his recitation of the rhyme, *Goodnight, God bless, go to bed and undress. Half the bed, half the clothes, lie on your back and you won't squash your nose.*

To enhance his image as local colour, when my father wasn't behind the wheel of some nondescript, sales rep's car or drab delivery van, he only ever drove convertibles. *Dropheads* he called them and he owned a succession of them - a Sunbeam Talbot, a Ford Zephyr Mark 1, a Ford Consul, an Austin Metropolitan, an Austin Ripley, a Triumph Herald.

If the roof folded down and made my dad look less like a married thirty-something with two young kids and more like a devil-may-care man about town then that was the motor for him.

He never paid more than £25 for any of them and drove each one into the ground before replacing it with the next, which was usually as battered but briefly more reliable than the last.

On Sundays, rain or shine but usually rain, the family would go for a drive. My mother, my big sister and I would sit huddled under rugs and coats, exposed to the elements. Behind the wheel sat dad, deerstalker at a rakish angle, pipe clenched between his teeth, monocle on a cord flapping uselessly round his neck. Sometimes we'd call in on family friends - mostly people dad had met when he'd been selling door-to-door. We'd arrive out of the blue, which was something you did in those days. No texting first or emailing. No declaring your intentions on Facebook or Twitter. No ringing on your mobile phone to say you're in the area and would it be OK to drop by? You'd just turn up. Imagine that.

Welcomed in and ushered through to the front room, the grown-ups would sit and chat while us kids played. Awkwardly. Awkwardly because these were kids we didn't see as often as our school friends or the boys and girls who lived next door or down the road. These were our parents' friends' kids. Their mum and dad knew our mum and dad. That was really all we had in common. Sometimes there would be a new toy to talk about or we'd make polite conversation about the latest episode of TV's *Billy Bunter*. But mostly we just sat there in silence. 'Why don't you children play outside?' would be a helpful suggestion from our parents, as if the fresh air would somehow loosen our tongues. I seem to remember the only time we took this advice, a boy called Roger threw half a brick at my head. At least the mild concussion meant a premature but welcome end to the misery of that particular afternoon.

If we didn't visit friends, our Sunday outings ended up at one of Somerset's military surplus dumps. We'd invariably arrive feeling a little light-headed, thanks to the petrol fumes that leaked from the car's aged and stuttering engine. We'd disembark and, led by dad, make our way towards some cavernous aircraft hangar. Once inside, my old man was as happy as a pig in muck, picking over mountains of decommissioned junk, convinced that in amongst the ammo boxes, kit bags and camp beds there would be something useful. Or ornamental.

Or something that, with a lick of paint and a bit of spit and polish, would make him some money.

As a consequence of these frequent shopping sprees our home and garden were littered with all manner of Army, Navy and Air Force paraphernalia.

Among my favourites was a camel-coloured duffle coat. Its weight and warmth comforted me in my bed on winter nights; nights when two blankets and a quilted eiderdown couldn't keep out the cold that, along with the eerie sound of the fog horns, crept in from Bristol's icy Channel.

I was also quite taken by a pair of six feet tall, fibre glass rocket nose cones. Dad kept them until his dying day; pointy, indestructible sore thumbs that stuck out everywhere he lived.

God only knows what he thought he'd ever do with them. 'They'll be worth something one day,' he reckoned.

But 'one day' was always tomorrow and, as everybody knows, tomorrow never comes. The fact is, rotten, rusted or busted, most things my father bought eventually turned to worthless dust. I often wonder if those rocket cones are still out there somewhere. Perhaps we should have tried to track them down and buried him in one of them. Saved the cost of a coffin. He'd have liked that, my dad. He liked saving money.

I also wonder what he would make of his 18 year old grandson in his over-priced, designer label, camouflaged combat trousers. There were plenty of the originals up for grabs at the army surplus store; perhaps the only thing that actually would have been worth something one day. And pretty much the only thing dad didn't buy.

So, am I a chip off the old block? The apple that didn't fall far from the tree? Am I my father's son?

I'm a Broome, there's no denying that. I have the family nose - a slight bump just below the bridge and a fleshy tip. I have the deep set eyes. And I have the curls that inexplicably deserted dad in his youth to be replaced by a head of hair as ramrod straight as it proved to be enduring. He kept it till the end, insisting, as he had done for at least 30 years before he died, that it was blonde not white. Did I mention that as well as being a bit of a character my dad was also rather vain?

I also have the Broome cough; the bark that dogged my father and his father before him all their lives. Theirs was was the result of a lifelong addiction to nicotine. My father had smoked for as long as I could remember. And he'd been trying to give up for just as long; a losing battle he fought to the bitter end. He tried everything. Going cold turkey, chewing gum, sucking an extra strong mint or a Fisherman's Friend. He tried dummy cigarettes made from shiny white plastic and stuffed with cotton wool soaked in menthol. He tried swapping ready-mades for roll-ups, hoping the laborious process of making a roll-up might at least slow down his habit. Then someone gave him a cigarette making machine; a small, silver box that spat out a perfectly formed roll-up almost as quick as you can say 'Have you got a light?'

And so another attempt to give up the gaspers disappeared in a puff of smoke. He tried acupuncture and hypnosis. Nothing worked. Towards the end of his life I told him the stress of trying to give up was more likely to kill him than his twenty a day habit.

As for my cough; my rattling, rasping call sign. Well, I suppose I had to inherit at least one family affliction. My poor old sister got the rest - the occasional allergic reactions, the mild bouts of eczema, the sinusitis, the varicose veins, the long sightedness that briefly condemned her to National Health specs in her teens, the mild deafness in later life.

And, married for the first time before I was 20 and for the third time before I was 40, I may have inherited some of my father's complicated feelings for women.

But a chip off the old block? 'Strike!' as he often exclaimed, I hope not.

He wasn't a bad person. Another of his sayings was *Consider others*. And he did. He really did.

He considered the deaf, dumb and blind. He considered the disabled and the children with Down's Syndrome. He considered the old and the lonely who were in need of a little cheer on Christmas Eve. He considered the kids - the teddy boys, the greasers and their girlfriends - who sat listless and bored in Burnham's Silver Lining Cafe. He considered the gypsies who appeared at our back door selling pegs. And he considered the turbaned Indians who crossed continents to find our little cottage in the middle of nowhere solely, it seemed, to persuade my dad to spend a week's housekeeping on flashy silk ties he'd never wear. He was even considerate towards stray cats and dogs.

He drummed his *Consider others* mantra into me and my sister. We'd often accompany him on his do-gooding missions. We went for walks on Burnham's beach holding hands with the boys and girls with cerebral palsy. We learned basic sign language so we could *talk* to the residents at the local home for the deaf. In the days just before Christmas we delivered parcels of tinned ham, canned fruit and homemade mince pies to those in need. It was a good thing to do but, honestly, I'd rather have been out playing with my mates.

And as I grew up and older I found myself unable to shake off the notion of *Consider others*. Eventually it became more of a burden than a blessing. Don't get me wrong. I am by no means a selfless person, but I can be out and about almost anywhere and if I see someone who isn't considering others I'm immediately irritated and distracted by it.

At a concert I can spot someone on the other side of the venue standing up and instantly I'm consumed by thoughts of how much that must be ruining things for the person sitting behind them. It shouldn't matter to me. My view isn't being obscured. I'm not the one who's paid £45 for the dubious pleasure of spending the night staring at someone's fat, jiggling arse. But still I can no longer concentrate on the gig. I'm constantly looking over to see if the offender has sat down yet.

The longer they stay standing up, the crosser I get and the more my evening is spoiled. On stage Kanye West could be joined by Paul McCartney, Lady Gaga and an animated hologram of Elvis Presley and I'd miss it all. I'd be too busy trying to catch the eye of the standing man so I could give him a look that says 'Consider others and sit down, you thoughtless git'. The person I'm *considering* is of course oblivious to all this. Judging by the look on their face, they're not bothered at all. They're having a great time.

Or I can be on holiday relaxing by the pool when I see a kid at the other end of the pool dive bombing. It's happening 50 metres away from me. I'm not getting splashed. I can't hear the smack as his curled up body hits the water. Over and over again. But still I'm annoyed. I'm seething with rage on behalf of all the people around him who I imagine are having their holiday ruined by this child's selfish behaviour. Though once again, none of them look remotely concerned. Chatting, reading, listening to music on their headphones, they're having a nice, relaxing holiday. It's only me who's getting wound up. It's only me who's wishing I wasn't here.

So, as a doctrine, *Consider others* has become something of a cross for me to bear. As for my dad, well, the biggest problem was while he was busy considering others - everyone from the crippled and the infirm to the rebels without a cause - he forgot about considering those who should have mattered to him most. Us. His wife and two children. And that's not nice. That's not a legacy I want.

CHAPTER 2

LIKE THE COMPACT FAMILY HATCHBACK

So, I was born on 16th November 1950 at the Mary Stanley Nursing Home in Bridgwater, Somerset. At the time I arrived, weighing a reasonably healthy few pounds and ounces, dad was working for the Kleen-Eze company, selling household cleaning products door to door. As a consequence, my birth certificate introduced me to the world with the words: Father's Surname - Broome. Father's Occupation - Brush Company Representative.

And it gets better.

Despite the fact that the recorded family address at the time was the Westfield Holiday Camp, Burnham-on-Sea, which sounds like I'd started life following a quick fumble and a knee-trembler behind one of the chalets, and despite the fact that my old man scraped a living selling dustpans and brushes from a cart he pulled along behind a bike, my given names were Leon Michael Auguste.

Leon Michael Auguste for Christ's sake!

My dad's idea of course. Did I mention he was a bit of a character? And when you're a bit of a character you don't call your son Alan or David or Robert. Oh no. Who did he think we were? Prussian nobility?

Actually, whilst we were definitely not of Prussian descent, there were all sorts of family stories about possible connections with nobility, even blue blood.

The Plantagenet kings and queens of England, for example. Apparently they wore sprigs of broom on their royal garments. Perehaps we were somehow related to that most powerful of dynasties; distant cousins of Henry II and his wife, Eleanor.

Or perhaps, by Royal Appointment, we were merchants to the court. Perhaps we made daily deliveries of freshly harvested broom to his and her highness and, given exclusive access to their chambers, perhaps we'd help them dress their robes of state. And, as valued suppliers, friends even, perhaps we would occasionally have joined Henry and Eleanor at the top table in the banqueting hall for a night of feasting, roistering and royal bacchanalia.

Or perhaps we just made brooms. From twigs. And gave them to other peasants - dirt poor, simple folk like us - in exchange for turnips and curly kale, so we could eat and they could sweep out their hovels.

Or perhaps not.

Regal lineage aside, for a while there was also talk of wealthy, if not noble, Swiss connections; whispered conversations about a sordid past involving rich relatives in the land of chocolate and cuckoo clocks. However, all hopes of a share in the Nestlé millions or the as yet unclaimed inheritance of some deceased Zurich gnome were dashed when a branch of the family tree revealed a connection with a young Swiss goat-herd who ran away from home to marry a penniless Welsh schoolteacher.

My mother's maiden name incidentally was Smitchd. Not to be confused with Schmidt, which it frequently is until, like Leon, like Broome, it's painstakingly spelled out.

Anyway, when the Second World War broke out, the name aroused suspicion behind the twitching curtains of Hall Green, the neighbourhood of Birmingham where my mum grew up. Overnight the friendly Brummie accents went from singsong to something altogether more sinister.

'Smitchd? Sounds German to me.'

The first whiff of tar and feathers in Reddings Lane and nan and grampy decided Mr. and Mrs. Smith might be a better name to see them through our spot of bother with Herr Hitler.

But back to Leon Michael Auguste.

When I questioned dad about his choices, 'Leon, after Leonardo da Vinci,' he said matter-of -factly, 'Michael after Michelangelo and Auguste after Auguste Rodin'.

Why couldn't I have been John after John Wayne, Roy after Roy Rogers and Gary after Gary Cooper?

Of course Michael wasn't really a problem - a common enough name and no-one needed to know its pretentious origins. And Auguste? Well, the subject of a third middle name rarely comes up before you're old enough to apply for a driving license or fill in a tax return.

But there was no escaping Leon. It was my bloody name and I had to deal with it.

As soon as I was old enough to be self-conscious about it, my mass of ginger curls and rash of freckles paled into insignificance (sadly not literally, but that's another story). I had one obsession and one obsession only - finding a way to make my name cool.

Remember, I grew up in the 50s and 60s - no *Kings of Leon* rocking out at the Glastonbury Festival in front of thousands; no groovy *Leon* restaurants and cookbooks; no *Leon* the rogue replicant in *Blade Runner* or *Leon*, the enigmatic hitman played by Jean Reno in the film of the same name - Leon, the professional you hired if you wanted 'a job done properly'. Even the *Seat Leon* would have been better than nothing. To anyone who struggled with my name I could have said 'Leon. Like the compact family hatchback'. Or maybe not.

As it was I scoured the credits of cowboy films and listened intently to the cast list of radio's *Journey Into Space* for Leons.

If I was to get any respect in the school playground I needed to share my name with a character who was rough and tough; a real he-man who always got the girl.

Each week I scrutinised the pages of my *Buster* comic hoping they'd introduce a new superhero - *Leon, Man of Steel*; *Leon,*

23

King of the Wild Frontier; *Leon, Ace of Spies*. I devoured books. Maybe, buried somewhere between the covers of *Captain Blood* or *Biggles Sees It Through* there was a Leon who was handsome and heroic.

If there was, I never found him.

I think I may have spotted someone called Leon Fromkess once, the name scrolling by at the end of *Fury*. Or was it *Hawkeye and the Last of the Mohicans*? Anyway, he was a producer or cameraman or something - not the image I was going for.

So, what to do?

When asked my name, one option was simply to mumble it - something, I'm afraid to say, I did well into adulthood. As a result, who knows how many brief encounters ended with me going one way and my short-lived acquaintance going theirs convinced my name was Ian, Liam or Neil. No harm done.

On one particular occasion, however, things did get a little out of hand. I was living in North London at the time and had a next door neighbour called Lal.

Meeting for the first time, my mumbled pronunciation and his slight deafness left him believing my name was Ian. I did try to correct him during various conversations in the weeks that followed, but in the end I took the line of least resistance. I went with Ian.

We exchanged pleasantries over the garden fence, me not batting an eyelid as he repeatedly referred to me as Ian. 'Looks like it might rain later Ian', 'How's work Ian?' and 'Big game at Highbury tonight Ian'.

Everything was going well until: 'I run this little jazz club down at the Kings Head, Ian. Why don't you come down and meet some of the lads?'

Without thinking I said yes and by three o'clock the next Sunday afternoon I had 50 new friends who all knew me as Ian. From that day forward I suffered an identity crisis every time I took a stroll down Crouch End Broadway.

CHAPTER 3

THE POWER OF HOODOO

There was a village school in Berrow, the Somerset village where I grew up. For reasons I never questioned, my parents didn't send me there. But I remember a small, single storey, grey stone building. I always imagined that inside there was just one classroom, dark, damp and crammed full of slack-jawed 4 to 11 years olds, monotonously reciting their times tables and learning by rote the rules of grammar. And in my mind's eye, watching over them was some hatchet-faced school ma'am, steel grey hair scraped up into a bun, beady eyes fixed in an unblinking stare. And in her hand I pictured a cane, ready to punish any poor mite who dared to stumble and stutter over the fact that i comes before e...EXCEPT AFTER C!

I knew a boy who went to Berrow Primary. I think his name was Christopher. He was a big, raw-boned boy with a mop of straw blonde hair and he wore National Health specs, usually with sticking plaster over the left lens.

National Health specs were an abomination universally loathed at of the time. They were either round with thin, wire rims coated in mock tortoiseshell or horn-rimmed, flesh-coloured plastic. This was years before designer glasses made being four-eyed fashionable and I can still see Susan Campbell at the school bus stop in hysterics, crying, screaming, stamping her foot and flatly refusing to get on the bus. Perched on her nose and splattered with tears were her brand new pair of National Health glasses and there was no way Susan was going to school wearing them. We left her behind in the end, she and her mum engaged in a sort of glasses on/glasses off double-act at the side of the road.

Anyway, Chris and I occasionally met on bike rides up to Heron House and the caravan park where, for a penny, you could buy a single sheet of bubble gum from a machine. The gum came with jokes that we'd swap on the ride home. Jokes like *What did the cannibals say to the stranger in town? We'd love to have you for dinner.* Or *Your teeth are like stars. They come out at night.* But we never swapped stories about our school life. So what actually went on behind the closed doors of Berrow Primary remained a mystery to me.

So instead of the village school, I went first to Princess Street and then St. Andrews, both in Burnham.

I don't remember how I got there, presumably on the No. 93 bus. But I do remember that in my last year at St. Andrews I cycled to and fro, occasionally slipstreaming the No. 93, riding dangerously close to its rear bumper in an attempt to impress the Bullock sisters - Marie and Sandra - who always sat in the back seat.

Talking of the Bullock sisters, one of my best friends at the time, Colin Dyer, developed a bit of a crush on Marie. We were out on our bikes one day when, from a distance, he spotted an opportunity to make his move.

27

The two girls were standing outside the secondhand furniture shop their parents ran in the village. Colin's plan was to gather up as much speed as he could before sweeping up to the shop. He'd skid to a dramatic halt, dismount and, emerging enigmatically from a cloud of roadside grit and gravel, he'd saunter up to Marie and with a casual nod introduce himself to the object of his desires. Impressed by his bicycling prowess and obvious athleticism, Marie would be instantly smitten.

I followed at a discreet distance as Col's cunning plan took shape.

Bent over his drop handlebars, he raced off. His little legs were a blur as he gathered speed with each frantic turn of the pedals. So far, so good. As he approached the shop, the two girls looked up. The stage was set for Colin's spectacular entrance. With just a few yards to go he slammed on the back brake. The rear wheel locked, triggering the start of an almighty skid, which Colin controlled with conspicuous skill. Again, so far, so good. The girls were transfixed as boy and bike hurtled towards them. Eventually, at precisely the spot where Marie was standing, Colin screeched to a standstill.

And that was the beginning of his downfall. Literally.

His feet were still locked in the toe straps on his pedals. The sheer speed of his manoeuvre hadn't given him enough time to trigger the quick release mechanism. Unable to put a foot down on the ground to steady himself, Colin simply toppled over, helplessly and hopelessly trapped in his bike.

Like a beetle on its back he just lay there.

Finally I arrived. I helped him up and dusted him down. Needless to say Colin's moment, not to mention his cool, was lost. As the two girls disappeared into their parents' shop, pausing just long enough to give us both a withering backward glance, Col and I got back on to our bikes and pedalled off. I glanced down and noticed he wasn't using his toe straps. They were Italian, top of the range. They'd cost him several weeks' worth of pocket money and he was particularly proud of them. But I didn't say a word.

Back to school.

I don't remember much about the day to day routine of those early years. I think I quite enjoyed it. I didn't struggle with the three Rs. I didn't excel at them either. I just got on with them as I recall.

Fuelled by our daily third of a pint of free school milk - always drunk straight from the bottle, always lukewarm in summer and barely above frozen in winter - playtimes went by in endless games of marbles, tig (sometimes known as 'it') or chain touch. Respite - time out to get your breath back or recover from the stitch - involved crossing your fingers and shouting 'Cree!'

There were also hours of fun to be had by asking other kids 'Are you a PLP?'

If they answered no, you'd recoil in mock horror. 'You're not a proper living person?'

Humiliated, they'd demand the question be repeated.

29

'OK, are you a PLP?' you'd ask obligingly.

'Yes,' they'd reply.

This was your cue to hurl yourself at them and lean on them heavily. 'Well, you did say you were a public leaning post'.

This hilarious catch 22 quizzing could go on all playtime.

So too could the legendary *You remind me of a man* duologue. It went like this…

'You remind me of a man'.

'What man?'

'A man of power'.

'What power?'

'The power of hoodoo'.

'Hoodoo?'

'You do'.

'Do what?'

'Remind me of a man'.

'What man?'

'A man of power...'.

You get the picture.

Apart from all this fun and games, two events stand out from my Princess Street years. One perhaps hinted at the shape of things to come and involved the tools of our artistic endeavours back in the 1950s - powder paint and sugar paper.

Basically everyone in the class was given the task of recreating a repeat pattern, as drawn on the blackboard by our teacher. It was a loopy and dotty kind of thing, which I've since discovered tests hand eye co-ordination skills.

Anyway, off we went. Or at least, off went my classmates.

I sat there, head cradled in my left hand, paintbrush in my right hand. I doodled aimlessly, albeit quite colourfully. When the time allotted to complete the task was up, we were invited to turn our paper over and do whatever we wanted on the other side. Everyone except me that is. I'd already done whatever I wanted, as the teacher pointed out with a disapproving shake of her head. So when I turned my paper over it was to attempt the repeat pattern.

Actually I made a pretty good job of it in the end and when some older boys and girls were invited to comment on the class's efforts, mine did rather well. My *abstract* on the reverse did less well. 'Don't know what that is.' being one piece of stinging criticism that still haunts me.

When I say it was an event that perhaps hinted at the shape of things to come, what I'm thinking of is an important geography exam a few years later. Along with one or two other instances, it was an occasion when, inexplicably and seemingly regardless of the consequences, I just drifted off into a world of my own.

The geography exam, for example, earned me a mark of 2%, something I must surely have seen coming when I handed in my paper. On it was my name, the day's date and a half-completed sentence about irrigation in the Indus Valley. But for reasons I can't fathom to this day, I couldn't have cared less.

The other memorable event from those Princess Street days involved a boy called Stephen and *Lady Chatterley's Lover.* Somehow Stephen had got hold of a copy of the book - his dad owned a pub so maybe had contacts. Anyway, we kids knew absolutely nothing about the literary merits of D.H. Lawrence's story, about its social criticism, its themes of individual regeneration and personal relationships. All we knew was it had some dirty bits in it.

So, when Stephen ushered a select gang of us boys into a quiet corner of the playground, we gathered round, buzzing with childish excitement, expecting an explosion of bad language, filthy and foul new words for everything from men's willies to ladies' front bottoms.

We were bitterly disappointed.

I vaguely remember something about 'cupping his balls', which briefly had us all sniggering, but not much else. Bored, as Stephen thumbed through page after page after page, one by one we drifted off and returned to our more innocent pastimes.

Having read the book since and, of course, appreciated its literary merits, its social criticism, its themes of individual regeneration and personal relationships, I now know the 'dirty bits' are in there. But at the time looking for them seemed like too much hard work. I'm not sure we'd have known what a 'cunt' was anyway.

CHAPTER 4

WORLD REFUGEE YEAR & THE GUN POWDER PLOT

In 1958 I left Princess Street Primary School and moved a few hundred yards up the road to St. Andrews Junior School.

Nothing much changed. The view was a bit better. St. Andrews was on the prom, opposite the pier (the shortest pier in the world apparently, and home to a motorised ride called Priscilla the Swan).

I was with mostly the same classmates.

We still did the three Rs. And we still drank our daily third of a pint of milk, though the older we got the harder it was to swallow. Our taste buds were moving on to more exciting sensations like squash and fizzy pop. Milk may have been helping us to build strong teeth and bones, but who cared? A glug of Corona orangeade was much more fun; the bubbles tickling your tongue and making you burp like a cow.

We still played marbles, tig and chain touch. And we swapped cards we'd collected from packets of Brooke Bond tea. There was a new theme every few months - everything from *British Wildlife* to *Out Into Space* - and each card was illustrated. The aim was to collect a complete set. This involved swapsies and a certain amount of negotiating. For example, you may have had to sacrifice a *Stoat*, a *Common Seal* and a *Long Eared Bat* just to get your hands on an *Eclipse Of The Moon*. But the satisfaction of finally filling up your *Out Into Space* album made the deal worthwhile.

Occasionally, inspired by the increasingly popular medium of something called 'television', we re-enacted scenes from our favourite cartoons. Like *Popeye The Sailor Meets Ali Baba's Forty Thieves*.

The school's outside toilets doubled as Abu Hassan's secret cave. I can remember riding into the toilet-cum-cave on my imaginary black stallion. Buttoned at the neck, I wore my school raincoat like a cloak and with my thieves galloping behind me, in my best *basso profondo* voice I sang 'I'm Abu Hassan'.

I can't remember who played Popeye - possibly Mark Stent. The pasty faced and slightly chubby Stephen, the pub landlord's son from Princess Street, was a natural Wimpy. Of course we had to manage without Olive Oyl. They were a couple of lanky 10 year old girls who definitely had the figure for it, but at playtime boys and girls were segregated.

So while we went about our fantastic adventures in one half of the playground, they had to make do with soppy stuff like skipping, hopscotch and French knitting in their half.

You had to feel sorry for them. Who wouldn't want to spend their playtime charging in and out of a school toilet, trying to avoid stepping into the remains of David Hunt's breakfast, most of which he'd spewed up and left on the floor after being punched in the stomach by some passing bully?

So, much like at Princess Street, school life went by pretty routinely. Although once again two or three significant events spring to mind when I look back on the years I spent at St. Andrews.

The first was World Refugee Year. Basically, almost 15 years after the end of the Second World War, many refugees still remained in camps. It was seen as a disgrace and the United Nations launched a programme to resolve the refugee problem once and for all. 1959-1960 was declared World Refugee Year and the aim was to 'clear the camps'. And it worked. By the end of 1960, for the first time since before the war, all the refugee camps in Europe were closed.

I only know this because I've checked since, but at the time I think all I knew was that we school kids had been asked to write a short story imagining what it must be like to be refugee.

I have no idea what I wrote. Or where I got my inspiration from. My family wasn't rich, actually we were quite hard-up, but we had a roof over our heads and three square meals a day. And I had a bicycle, a cowboy outfit, a Davy Crockett hat, some boxing gloves and a clockwork train set (all either home-made or secondhand, but still). So we weren't exactly living the refugee life.

Anyway I wrote my story, handed it in to *Miss* and thought no more about it.

A few weeks later I was out playing by the church on the golf links when the vicar - the Reverend Wright - called me over. 'It's Leon Broome, isn't it?' he said.

I nodded, slightly anxious. We weren't churchgoers and I thought the Rev might be about to try and convert me. Dad, having long since passed through his fire and brimstone phase, was now a militant atheist and had taught me to be suspicious, not to say dismissive, of anything and anyone involved with religion.

'I've just heard your short story on the wireless...the refugee story,' said the vicar. 'Well done...very well done indeed'. And with that he jumped in his Morris Minor Traveller and drove off.

I had no idea what he was talking about. I remembered writing the story of course, but what was it doing being read out on the BBC's Home Service? I raced back home and asked mum and dad if they had any idea what was going on. They knew about as much as me.

A couple of days later a typewritten envelope dropped through our letterbox. It was addressed to Master Leon Broome. I don't think I'd received a typewritten letter before and I wasn't sure what to make of it. I stood staring at it, reading my name and address over and over again. 'Master L. Broome, Church Cottage, Berrow, Burnham-on-Sea, Somerset. Master L. Broome,

Church Cottage, Berrow, Burnham-on-Sea, Somerset. Master L. Broo…'.

Eventually mum said something: 'Well, I think we've established who it's for. Now I think we need to find out who it's from, don't you?'

I opened the envelope and looked inside.

'It's a letter,' I said.

'No kidding,' said my big sister, with thinly disguised sarcasm.

I took out the letter and unfolded it. It was on World Refugee Year headed paper and with it was a cheque for 10/6d - about £25 in today's money. The letter explained it was my prize for penning the winning story in their competition. But it didn't say much else.

I don't know if we tried to find out more at the time. I've certainly tried since. But although World Refugee Year is well documented, there's no mention anywhere of Leon Broome and his early brush with fame.

The next event still makes my blood run cold when I think about it.

It was the gun powder plot. Nothing to do with Guy Fawkes, 1605 and all that, it was a plan hatched by Terry Keirle and I and our intention was not to assassinate a king but to give our new and hated headmaster a nasty surprise.

Sir smoked a pipe, which he frequently left in his desk drawer during break. Our plan was simple. With *Sir* otherwise engaged on playground duty, we'd go to his desk, take out the pipe and fill it with gun powder we'd got from a penny banger.

Sometime later, he'd light his pipe, there'd be a flash and when the smoke cleared he'd look like one of those cartoon characters who's just lit up an exploding cigar - singed eyebrows, blackened face, smouldering hair. Hilarious but, like in the cartoons, no harm done. He'd live to teach another day.

After discussing the finer details - who would get the gunpowder, which one of us would plant the explosive while the other kept watch - we laid our booby trap the following lunchtime.

It failed.

Sir didn't suddenly appear later that day or any other day, singed around the edges. I guess he must have tapped out his pipe, like pipe smokers often do, before filling it with fresh tobacco and lighting up. Thank God. I look back now and think that if everything had gone according to plan we could have blown the poor man's face off. Or at least blinded him. We'd probably still be in prison.

The third event I remember was the one and only fight I've ever had. It was with a boy called Eddie. I don't know what started it - possibly I'd asked him if he was a PLP - but as we squared up to each other we were instantly surrounded by a circle of other small boys yelling 'Fight! Fight! Fight!'

Striking the traditional pose of a prizefighter about to engage in the noble art of pugilism - Grampy Broome had been a boxer in the Royal Navy - I was about to explain to Eddie that we should observe Marquess of Queensberry rules.

But before I could get a word out about no punching below the belt or breaking on the referee's command, he'd charged at me, got me in a head lock and wrestled me to the ground.

I was only saved from a severe pummelling by the timely arrival of the headmistress who grabbed Eddie by the scruff of his grey school jumper and pulled him off me. Gathering me into her skirt, she gently led me to the safety of the staff room.

Halfway across the playground I'd looked back through my tears. Eddie, clenched fists raised above his head, was being held aloft by his friends, champion of all he surveyed. I silently vowed to get my revenge one day.

Of course, I never did.

However, a couple of years later I did discover that Eddie was one of the kids who lived in the children's home on Burnham's sea front. I didn't know his circumstances - orphaned, abandoned or taken into care to protect him from some terrible domestic abuse - but I did feel sorry for him and put the beating he gave me down to his anger at the world and nothing personal.

Actually, there is one other event I vividly remember from my St. Andrews days.

We didn't have a dining room at school, so every lunchtime we'd form up in twos and snake our way through the town to a hall opposite Burnham's Manor Gardens. On arrival we'd take our seats at tables of ten - girls on the left hand side of the hall, boys on the right. The table leader, usually someone from Form 4, sat at one end, his second in command at the other and we'd wait to be called up to the serving hatch, table by table, to get our lunch.

One day, while my table was waiting, our leader, Johnny, decided to exercise his authority. He ordered a boy called Jeffrey to drink our entire allocation of water. In one go. Jeff had no choice but to obey. Johnny was handy (and free) with his fists. His mum was also a teacher at St. Andrews, which seemed to give him extra powers and privileges.

So the rest of us sat watching, with a mixture of admiration and apprehension, as tumbler by tumbler Jeff downed an entire jugful of water - four or five pints by my reckoning. He looked a bit bloated by the end but still happy enough to go up for his school dinner and wolf it down, pudding and all, with his usual enthusiasm.

It was only when the time came to go that we noticed all was perhaps not well. As soon as Jeff stood up he looked a little green around the gills. He was wobbly on his feet and his stomach was noticeably swollen. Under the increased pressure, a button popped off his shirt and flew across the dining room.

His tummy began to rumble ominously. It began to quiver and shake. Sweat started pouring down his face. It was as if all that water was literally leaking out of him.

The teachers realised something was up. 'Stand back everyone!' they shouted.

'Stand back! He's gonna blow!' shrieked one of the dinner ladies, retreating to a safe distance.

And that was when it happened.

With a roar that rattled the hall's windows, Jeff opened his mouth and released an almighty wall of water. A foaming tsunami washed across the floor and lapped at our shoes. Mary Cooke fainted. A gaggle of terrified first years began paddling frantically towards the door. Next to me Colin Major started retching. It was like Niagara Falls gushing out of Jeff's gaping gob. Niagara Falls with peas, diced carrots and, unless I was very much mistaken, a little bit of jam roly-poly.

CHAPTER 5

THE MUNTS, THE CHICKS, THE NIBLETTS & THE GIBLETTS

I don't know if it's a coincidence or a heightened sense of awareness sparked by my own slightly unusual handle (Broome. Handle. Geddit?) but odd names have been a theme throughout my life.

I had an Uncle Einar, allegedly christened to honour a promise Grampy Broome made to name his first born after the Norwegian sailor who saved his life at the Battle of Jutland. Despite its heroic origins it just made me giggle because it sounded like anus. I had cousins called Pinches and a friend called Pauline Want, who actually was quite demanding, particularly when it came to me taking the male role in endless renditions of *Soldier Soldier Won't You Marry Me?* There was Gloria Prout who thought about calling her son Russell until someone pointed out he'd be Russell Prout; just two consonants away from being named after the quintessential Christmas dinner veg. In the end she went for Steven. S. Prout. Much better. And in later life I'd encounter R. Donn aka Dick Donn (whichever way you look at it, just plain rude), Prosper Dowden and Marlene Haddock to name but a few.

But, perhaps best of all, while I was still agonising over what to do about being Leon Michael Auguste, we were joined in our Somerset village by some new neighbours. Four families in all, who took up residence in the newly built terrace of pebble-dashed council houses just a few yards down the road. Immediately next door to us were Mr. and Mrs. Munt and their two children, next door to them were Mr. and Mrs. Chick and family, then Mr. and Mrs. Niblett and their brood and, in the last house, Mr. and Mrs. Giblett and their two daughters.

Suddenly, being a Broome didn't seem so bad.

The arrival of the four new families in our Somerset outpost brought with it another bonus - kids my own age on the doorstep. I had school friends, boys like Mark Stent, Terry Keirle and Graham Bartlett (who I bumped into after 20 years apart and whose first words to me were not 'Long time no see' or 'I recognise that face' but 'Oright, spunk bubble'.)

The problem was most of my classmates lived at least a three mile cycle ride away.

It wasn't necessarily too far for my skinny little legs to carry me, but I was frequently put off by the million miles an hour headwinds that seemed to blow relentlessly on our particular stretch of the Somerset coastline – there was only so much battering I was prepared to take, even for my best friends.

Closer to home was the aforementioned Colin Dyer. Long before the Bullock sisters incident, we'd connected over a cub scouts uniform which I'd inherited from him after he'd grown out of it. I quite liked Cubs. The woggle, the dyb-dyb-dybbing, Akela with her soft cheeks faintly rouged like my favourite auntie's and the comforting scent of her 4711 eau de cologne.

The scouts, on the other hand, I did not enjoy.

I only went once and we played British Bulldogs. Far too rough. Give me flower pressing or a leisurely visit to the Axbridge Waterworks any day.

Although one thing I didn't like about Cubs was *Bob A Job Week*.

Basically, it was young boys in tight fitting green jumpers accessorised by sunshine yellow neck-scarves, knee socks and short trousers. Matching caps at a cheeky angle, we were sent out unaccompanied to knock on strangers' doors and offer to do their bidding for the princely sum of *a bob* - one shilling (5p). Surely that was asking for trouble.

If nothing else it was slave labour. Child slave labour at that.

I once spent the best part of a day weaving a network of string to and fro over what seemed to me to be mile after mile of newly sown lawn seed. 'To stop the birds eating it,' hissed some toothless old pensioner, before giving me a shilling and grudgingly signing my *Job Well Done* card. I also cleaned and polished a whole household's collection of shoes and boots and washed cars till the skin on my hands was red raw.

By the time *Bob A Job Week* came around again, I'd decided it was a mugs game.

So I persuaded my mum to let me do tasks around the house - a bit of light dusting here, peeling some potatoes there. I managed to pretty much fill up my card and hand over a few shillings to

Akela at the end of the week, without getting my hands dirty or working my fingers to the bone.

But I have to say the experience of *Bob A Job Week* left me scarred. I actually blame the Cubs and *Bob A Job Week* for my lifelong aversion to physical labour.

Returning to Colin.

He was at boarding school during term time. (Among Colin's classmates was a boy who'd shat himself on his first day. He was instantly branded *Shit*, a nickname which apparently stuck, as shit tends to, right up until the poor kid finally left school - and I thought I had problems being called Leon).

Anyway, with Colin away a lot of the time, the arrival of Joe and Isobel Chick, the youngest Niblett, Robert, and the Giblett girls, Monica and Brenda, meant I had someone I could easily call for and ask to come out and play. Though I have to say it was not always with my parents' blessing.

The new arrivals were, heaven forbid, council house types - not quite the company mater and pater wanted their brillianteened boy to keep. Yes, the Chicks et al were Somerset to their core and said things like *bain't* and *casn't* instead of *not* and *can't*. It was a habit I picked up with relish, if only to annoy my parents and, in particular, undermine dad's delusions of grandeur.

So, call for them I did and the golf links across the road from where we all lived was our adventure playground. After-school hours and weekends were spent thrashing around the course with cut-down clubs or searching the rough for lost balls which we'd then clean and sell to passing golfers - quite possibly the same golfers who'd lost them in the first place. We'd retrieve prams dumped in ditches or at the roadside and use the wheels so we could make box carts to race up and down the hilly fairways and dunes.

Using choppers spirited away from our fathers' sheds, us boys would make clearings in the gorse bush jungles, dig holes six foot square and create underground dens where we'd sit drinking water flavoured with wine gums (we were convinced that was how wine was made) and giggling at pictures of women in Playtex girdles; pictures we'd hungrily torn from our mothers' mail order catalogues.

Making our way back from one particular den building expedition, Robert Niblett and I were carrying Joe Chick when Isobel, Joe's twin sister, approached us from across the fairway.

'What's happened?' she said.

'Joe's dead,' I replied, poker faced. 'Robert accidentally hit him with a spade'.

Isobel was instantly hysterical; inconsolable until eventually Joe opened his eyes and laughed like a drain.

A box of matches carelessly discarded by a parent or older brother was our ticket into the thrilling world of arson. I dread to think how many acres of gorse we laid waste with our fires or how much wildlife was sent scurrying before the advancing flames of our incendiary exploits.

Another less dramatic pursuit was to go out after dark and turn off the sprinklers the greenkeepers had set to water the greens overnight. The sound of the sprinkler's motor stuttering to a halt as we ran away was quite exciting. But it was never up there with the adrenalin rush of watching a fire roaring up a hillside quicker than you could say 'Call the fire brigade!'

In fact the fires we started were all pretty harmless and actually fitted in with the greenkeepers' own slash and burn approach to golf links management - that's my story anyway and I'm sticking to it.

Also pretty harmless, but hours of fun, was a dog turd carefully placed in the hole of a green. From a safe distance we'd watch as some poor, unsuspecting golfer sank a 20 yard putt. Whooping with glee at his achievement, he'd race to the hole and with a triumphant flourish plunge his hand in to retrieve his ball. It was with a less than triumphant flourish that he'd withdraw hand and ball covered in crap and stinking to high heaven. Only the sound of muffled giggles from the other side of a nearby hillock may have made him wonder if he was the victim of something other than a dog with a remarkably good aim.

Golfers were mostly toffs in those days. That they had more money and privileges than us didn't bother us kids, but we did resent them interrupting our fun and games on the fairway with their shouts of 'Fore!' and their angrily shaking fists. But that didn't stop Colin and I from turning up at the clubhouse and offering our services as caddies.

You could earn five shillings - 25p - for simply pulling a trolley around 18 holes. That was good money for a 12 or 13 year old in the early 1960s. I went out on several occasions with another caddy, an Irishman who I only ever knew as Mr. Baker.

Wreaking of alcohol, he'd sweat and pant his way round, a full bag of clubs weighing heavily on his shoulders (it was a matter of pride amongst the older caddies that they didn't use a trolley) and at every opportunity he'd sidle up to me, tap the side of his nose with his forefinger and with a knowing wink he'd whisper: 'Mr. Baker says a man never worries, a man never cares, he's just like a fuckin' tinker selling his fuckin' wares'.

At the time I didn't know what he meant. Now I'm older and wiser, I still don't.

I've already mentioned my lifelong aversion to physical labour and whilst wheeling a trolley round an 18 hole golf course, usually at the walking pace of a pensioner, isn't exactly physical labour, on one occasion I was nonetheless overwhelmed by my disinclination to overdo things.

We were on the 10th hole with 8 still to go. I was beginning to tire. The tee was quite high up and then the fairway dropped away down a steep hill. The elderly gentleman I was caddying for had driven off then tottered on ahead of me and out of sight. As I approached the top of the hill I saw my opportunity. I could take a much needed break from pulling the trolley simply by letting it freewheel down the hill. I'd keep pace with it of course; walk alongside it just in case I needed to stop it running away from me.

So I let go of the handle and waited for the trolley to make its leisurely way down the slope.

Except it didn't.

I'd no sooner let go of the handle than the whole trolley tipped up. Clubs and spare balls slid out of the bag and went skidding down the hill, followed by a brightly coloured, folded umbrella.

Worse, the trolley's handle snapped clean off.

Briefly I thought about running away and hiding in the bushes. But then I remembered how nice the old man had been. We'd chatted about school and hobbies and about how he was looking forward to getting home later that night and having a *gin and chronic* with his wife, who he'd been happily married to for 47 years.

My father's words came back to haunt me. *Consider others*. I couldn't do it. I called out.

'Er, I'm really sorry but…something's happened'. 'Help,' I added feebly.

After what seemed like an eternity, the old man reappeared over the brow of the hill. I pointed helplessly at the tangle of golfing accessories and equipment sprawled around and about.

Even from where I was standing - 20 or 30 yards away - I could see he'd closed his eyes, perhaps hoping that when he opened them again everything would be back to normal.

But when he did, it wasn't.

Eventually he trudged back up the slope and together and without speaking we collected the clubs, the spare balls and the brightly coloured, folded umbrella and put them back in the bag. He didn't ask what had actually happened. And I didn't tell him.

Its handle broken off, the trolley was no longer a functioning trolley. I was just a kid and he was an old man and, to be honest, not that strong judging by the way some of his drives dribbled off the tee.

There was nothing else for it. We'd have to share the burden of the clubs, the spare balls and the brightly coloured, folded umbrella, not forgetting the broken trolley, all the way back to the clubhouse.

It was very kind of him and he manfully played the remaining 8 holes in between helping me carry everything.

I was able to lighten the load a bit by dropping the trolley off at my house as we passed. I said I'd get it fixed and a couple of weeks later I delivered it to the clubhouse as good as new. I think the old chap may even have paid me for mending it.

I shared the whole sorry experience with Colin, who saw it as a business opportunity. We were already selling golfers their own balls, what about *accidentally* breaking their trollies and then fixing them for a fee?

'Consider others, Colin,' I said, 'Consider others'.

'Consider this, you ginger wazzock,' was his carefully considered response as he gave me a carefully considered Chinese burn.

CHAPTER 6

HANDS OFF BERROW

As I've already said, being so close, the golf course was the setting for most of our adventures, perhaps the most dramatic of which involved saving Britain from invasion.

We were gathered on the grassy bank outside Joe Chick's house. It was the same grassy bank from where I had wolf whistled at PC John Nimmo as he glided by on his whispering Velocette motorcycle. And the same grassy bank where, red faced in front of my friends, I had subsequently received a lecture on public order offences. I have to say I always suspected Constable Nimmo's indignation had more to do with the fact that my sister had refused to go out with him than with teaching me respect for the law.

It wasn't actually the first time wolf whistling had got me noticed, if not into trouble.

Some weeks before I'd wolf whistled at a friend of my sister's in Burnham high street.

I was a 10 year old boy. She was a 16 year old girl. Passers-by didn't know whether to laugh or ring the police. I don't know what I was thinking of, but I do know I loved whistling. I whistled here, there and everywhere. So omnipresent was my whistling, my parents were often approached by people who said they'd seen, or rather heard me and how my whistling had brightened up their day.

Sadly, in my opinion, whistling has gone out of fashion. Will we ever see the likes of Ronnie Ronalde - The Yodelling Whistler - again? Or whenever we feel afraid, will we hold our head erect and whistle a happy tune so no one will suspect we're afraid? I doubt it. I occasionally still purse my lips, puff out my cheeks and give a little toot. But no-one appreciates it. Everyone's too busy listening to bloody Stormzy on their smart phones.

Anyway, Colin, Robert, Joe and I were lounging around at the scene of my run in with PC Nimmo when Joe drew our attention to a Volkswagen Camper van he'd spotted parking by the church across the road. Four or five people got out and, laden down with rucksacks, set out across the golf links heading towards the beach.

'They're not from around here,' noted Colin, his eyes narrowing with suspicion.

'And that's a German car,' said Robert, who knew about these things because his older brother, Dennis, was a mechanic.

'Fifth columnists...the enemy within...secret ops,' intoned Joe, who on a recent visit to the dentist had read *Captain Hurricane* in *The Valiant,* so he knew what he was talking about too.

No more needed to be said.

Careful to keep out of sight, we trailed them. Eventually they approached one of the Second World War pillboxes that dotted the coastline. It had a newly installed door. Unlocking it, our quarry disappeared inside. Our imaginations were running wild. Nazis? Obviously. Spies? Of course. The nation in imminent danger? Absolutely no doubt about it.

There was no time to alert the authorities. By the time one of us had got back to the phone box in the village, rang the police station in Burnham-on-Sea and by the time Constable Nimmo had ridden the three miles from Burnham, parked his motorcycle and plodded across the dunes, Blighty could be overrun by the Hun.

No, we had to act now.

None of us fancied actually tackling the jerries. They all looked quite big - even the women - and they were almost certainly armed with machine guns, Lugers and quite possibly hand grenades.

So we decided to play a waiting game.

Hopefully they'd leave the pillbox soon - maybe to lay some mines along the shoreline. Then we brave few would seize the moment, storm their unmanned base, smash it up and thwart their evil intent.

And sure enough, after about half an hour they left.

It was better than we had hoped for. They were heading back towards the church. It looked like their plotting was over, for today at least. We'd have all the time in the world to carry out our plan. We watched them disappear into the distance and once we were sure they weren't coming back we launched our assault.

Joe, being the smallest, climbed in through one of the pillbox's windows. Releasing the catch on the door, he let the rest of us in. Grim faced, we looked around. Instantly our worst fears were confirmed. There were maps on the walls. Routes were marked out in livid red ink. There were lists - mysterious combinations of numbers and letters and code names like Skua, Kittiwake and Storm Petrel. There were aerial photographs in grainy black and white.

There was no doubt in any of our tiny minds that this was a plan of attack.

We set about destroying everything. But not before we'd raided the supply cupboard, fired up the primus stove and rustled up a snack of fried bacon and eggs. An army, after all, marches on its stomach.

We never saw the 'Nazis' again. And the trashed pillbox was abandoned. Mission accomplished. A few weeks later I overheard Mrs. Maisey in the village shop talking about some poor bird watchers whose hide had been vandalised by mindless idiots. She said maps of the local seabirds' migration paths had been trampled into the dirt, lists of birds the watchers had ringed to help track their movements had been torn to shreds, photos of nesting sites destroyed. Apparently the hooligans had even burnt a frying pan.

I was unmoved. I remained convinced I'd done my duty. I'd done my bit. I'd helped save my country.

I also like to think I did my bit to save our village. Not that it was under any immediate threat from property developers or road builders or out of town shopping centres. But Colin and I decided to err on the side of caution and let everyone know that the leafy lanes and wide open spaces of Berrow were not up for grabs.

We took our lead from the anti-Vietnam war protesters of the time. On both sides of the Atlantic, *Hands Off Vietnam* was daubed on walls and buildings everywhere. Admittedly, as a call to action it wasn't really working - the war, already nearly a decade old, would rumble on for another 12 years - but as a sentiment the message only needed to be slightly adapted to suit our purpose.

And so it was that late one summer's evening, under cover of darkness, Colin and I approached the red brick wall of the stable block next door to Berrow's ancient and picturesque St Mary's Church. In whitewashed, capital letters big enough for everyone to see, we scrawled our words of warning - *HANDS OFF BERROW.*

In the cold light of the next day, the good people of Berrow were scandalised.

Worshippers, arriving for Sunday service, questioned what the world was coming to. In the weeks that followed, the baker, the butcher, the milkman and the paperboy went about their deliveries tut-tutting and shaking their heads in disbelief at this blot on our picture postcard landscape. Even Joe, Robert and the rest, who weren't in on the act, said whoever was responsible had gone too far.

I don't think Colin and I ever spoke about the graffiti again. He may have taken our secret to his grave - sadly he died a few years ago - but I don't think he'd mind me owning up now.

And the fact is it worked.

The property developers and road builders and out of town shopping centres did keep their hands off Berrow. For a couple of years anyway. Then it was buried beneath an avalanche of bungalows, housing estates, mini roundabouts and convenience stores.

Still, at least we tried.

Another highlight of the school holidays was the Harvest Home - a kind of cross between a fete and a fun fair. It took place every year - in August I think - in a field just a couple of minutes' walk from where we all lived. And the first sign of its imminent arrival was the erection of a massive marquee.

Once the Harvest Home was declared open by the vicar, this tent, nestling in tranquil meadowland surrounded by trees and wild flowers in full bloom, became the setting for some of the bloodiest and most fiercely fought battles since Sedgemoor.

In other words, it was the setting for the annual *Burnham and Berrow Village Show*.

And hell was unleashed.

In the white heat of a tent in high summer, it was leek against leek, beetroot against beetroot, spud against spud. Scone squared up to scone and Victoria sponge waged war with Victoria sponge until one of them emerged, well, victorious. Chutney challenged chutney, jams were judged and babies were mercilessly compared to decide which was the most beautiful.

It rarely ended happily.

Sore losers could be heard muttering about bribery, blackmail and dark arts like the illegal use of growth hormones (for the plants of course not the babies. Although one year there were rumours about a particularly bonnie baby called Janet).

There was talk of bias bought for the price of a pint in the Berrow Inn. Gossip too of sexual favours offered in return for a rosette. And it's possible. Mrs. P, who my mother described as 'All fur coat and no knickers', did seem to win a disproportionate number of prizes for cakes and bakes that looked suspiciously shop bought.

In the aftermath of the judges' decisions friendships were often destroyed and lifelong neighbours left never speaking to each other again.

And all because one man's carrot was judged to be bigger than another's.

None of that interested us kids. All we cared about was the marquee itself. The minute it was up it became a gigantic canvas mountain crying out to be scaled. Over and over again, we'd scramble and claw our way to the top then slide down, squealing like stuck pigs. And stuck pigs were what two or three of us nearly became one afternoon. Joe Chick decided it would be fun to go inside the marquee and, using one of the spiked wall poles, stab at us as we slipped and skidded down the outside. After Colin came close to being pierced, Joe came close to being murdered. By Colin.

CHAPTER 7

VERY QUIET FOR A JEW

As well as acts of heroism in the face of an invading army and clandestine acts of protest, it was around this time that I started taking guitar lessons. My father had bought my big sister a Spanish guitar. (My sister, by the way, is Katina not Katrina. That would have been too easy and nowhere near characterful enough for dad. And being Katina not Katrina means that she, like me, has had a lifetime of spelling her name every time she introduces herself. Oh, the wasted hours).

Anyway, my father had bought my sister a Spanish guitar, hoping perhaps she would join him in the occasional rendition of *Hang Down Your Head Tom Dooley* or *Sipping Cider Through A Straw*. But Katina not Katrina showed no interest in playing Miki to dad's Griff or Nina to his Frederik.

So, I commandeered the guitar. Not because I wanted to be dad's partner in crimes against the popular folk songs of the day, but because I wanted to write pop music.

I had lessons in the village from Miss Evelyn Maude of *Miss Evelyn Maude's Gypsy Orchestra*. While I had my sights set on being the next Tommy Steele, the slightly scatty Miss M seemed more interested in turning me into the next Django Reinhardt. But among the arpeggios, the apoyandos and the legatos, I was learning a few chords, It was enough to convince me I was ready to write my first number one hit.

It was called *Tweedledeedee and Tweedledeedum* and the opening line was *Tweedledeedee and Tweedledeedum were two big giants who were having some fun*. It was a sure fire smash. I just needed to get it in front of a publisher.

I jotted down a couple of names and addresses copied from some sheet music Miss Maude had bought me. I think even she saw the writing was on the wall for the gypsy orchestra sound and was teaching me some instrumentals by an up and coming instrumental combo called The Shadows. I figured their publishers obviously knew a thing or two about pop and would recognise my talent when they saw it.

I carefully wrote out the lyrics on a page torn from a school exercise book - the melody was still in my head, but I told myself we'd sort that out once the contract was signed. Give too much away now and I could be ripped off by the 'fat bloated Jew boys' who my dad said ran show business.

Did I mention that as well as being a bit of a character and rather vain, my dad was also prone to the occasional bout of casual racism? It was more misguided than malicious. He's the only person I've ever known who saw the expression (and forgive me for this) 'big buck n****r' as a compliment. He used it once when he was describing a kitchen porter he worked with at the Langham Hotel in London's West End. The 'big buck n****r' in question had tried to strangle my father (that's why his Adam's apple stuck out apparently) and when dad told the story it was with a misty eyed fondness and obvious respect for his attacker. He really didn't see the expression as an insult or racial slur.

He also clung on to the notion of the *noble savage* pretty much until he died and I can't tell you how disappointed he was when he came to visit me in London and saw black men and women wearing shell suits and trainers. This was not how it was in *King Solomon's Mines*.

Anyway, I prepared to submit the first of what I anticipated would be a long line of pop hits.

There it was, writ large across the top of the page - *Tweedledeedee and Tweedledeedum* by Leon Broome. Shit! By who? Leon Broome! What sort of a name is that for a pop songwriter?

As I've already said, this was the '50s going on '60s. A man called Larry Parnes – Mr. Parnes, Shillings and Pence - was the pop impresario *du jour* and his stable of artists included Marty Wilde, Billy Fury, Duffy Power and Vince Eager. With names like that were they going to record something written by Leon Broome? I don't think so. I needed a new name; something catchy; something rock 'n' roll. Something, if dad was to be believed, Jewish.

I came up with Chris Costelloe.

I thought it sounded Jewish. The irony of my real name sounding actually quite Jewish didn't strike me until many years later when, after a noisy and drunken night out, some work colleagues observed that up until that moment they had thought I was very quiet for a Jew.

Anyway, I was convinced the name Chris Costelloe would open doors on Tin Pan Alley.

It didn't.

Tweedledeedee and Tweedledeedum came back time and again, accompanied by rejection slips in oddly extravagant typefaces. But no amount of serifed curlicues could disguise the fact that Chris Costelloe was a flop.

Undeterred, I wrote a second song - *Devil in Disguise*. I can't quite remember the lyrics, but I do remember rhyming *disguise* with *eyes* and possibly *lies*.

More importantly, I dumped Chris Costelloe and replaced him with Dobbs. Not someone Dobbs or Dobbs someone, just Dobbs. I even created a signature - they'd probably call it a logo now - with the tail of the s flicking back to underline the D, o, b and b. It was going to look brilliant at the bottom of my contract, not to mention in all those autograph books. For now it just looked mightily impressive at the top of my latest pop masterpiece - *Devil in Disguise* by Dobbs.

Off it went to a number of carefully selected publishers. I remember Dick James Music and Northern Songs were among the privileged few hand-picked to be blessed with the gift of my songwriting genius.

Maybe it was the slightly ill-formed and immature handwriting. Maybe it was the ruled paper. Maybe it was the overly optimistic covering letter offering them - at a mutually agreeable fee to be negotiated - exclusive rights to my next six compositions. Whatever it was, *Devil in Disguise* was returned to me accompanied not by offers of wealth beyond my wildest dreams but by more of those now familiar rejection slips.

I took some comfort from the fact that it wasn't actually me who was being rejected, it was Dobbs.

What did he expect with a bloody stupid name like that?

CHAPTER 8

SEXEY BEAST

Turning my back on the fickle world of show business, I threw myself into my school work. I'd passed my 11-plus and was now at grammar school. Of course I wasn't at any old grammar school with a run of the mill name like Bishops or Dr. Morgan's or North Somerset.

No, the gods of comedy names had selected Sexey's School for me.

In fairness, Sexey's School was well known in Somerset and mention of the name didn't automatically bring on a fit of giggles. Although, if I'd been around in the 16th century and been introduced to the school's benefactor, Hugh Sexey, even I, Leon Michael Auguste Broome, might have found it difficult to keep a straight face. But no, the name Sexey's School went largely unremarked upon in Somerset.

However, move 100 miles away to the Isle of Wight, change schools at the tender age of 13 and turn up for your first day wearing your former school's blazer, complete with a badge that says 'Sexey's School' and you get a slightly different reaction.

But I'll come to that later.

There were two Sexey's Schools in Somerset. The one I attended was (and remains) on the Somerset Levels, just outside the tiny village of Blackford. Founded in the late 19th century, it was small for a grammar school, even by the time I arrived in September 1961. And it had an excellent reputation. For the parents of most kids who'd passed their 11-Plus it was their first choice, but spaces were limited to a select few. I'll never know what swung it for me. I remember being quizzed at my interview about something called *sand couch* - a species of grass I later learned - and that my response was 'I don't get you'. I also remember thinking 'And I won't get a place at Sexey's after that performance'.

But a few weeks later an offer came through.

I immediately got in touch with my St.Andrews schoolmates - Terry, Graham, Mark and the rest of the gang - to see who else would be joining me. No-one. No-one at all from St.Andrews in fact, apart from a girl called Mary Cooke. So there'd be no familiar faces to help settle those first day at big school nerves.

I can't recall much about that first day. Dad, I guess, dropped me off at the Berrow Triangle - pick-up point for school bus. I waited outside Horsey the Butchers with another boy in Sexey's school uniform. He was older, bigger and we didn't speak. When the bus arrived we were the first to get on, so at least I avoided the embarrassment of all eyes on the new kid in his cap, short trousers and shiny new blazer.

The bus went through Berrow, on to Burnham and Highbridge, filing up with boys and girls as it went. No-one seemed to notice me, which was a relief. Even Mary Cooke walked straight past me, lost I imagine in her own anxious thoughts.

After the last pick up in Highbridge the bus began wending its way through the Somerset countryside. The whole journey - stops and starts included - took around 45 minutes.

And, as I would discover, our bus was the first to arrive in the morning and the last to leave after school. It was a long day, made even longer when I started cycling to and from the bus stop. I still don't think I've got over it, which may explain my enduring need to take regular afternoon naps - something I've done even at work where, in my experience, a toilet cubicle and a plump roll of toilet tissue is all you need to create a surprisingly comfortable place to grab 40 winks.

Anyway, starting at Sexey's was a milestone in my life, but like I say I really can't recall much about that first day. Or the days that followed, but eventually I must have settled in because what memories I have of those days are largely fond ones.

Academically, I took up where I left off at St. Andrews. I didn't excel nor did I struggle.

And though I can't remember how or why, I quickly made friends with three other boys - Philip Stone, Gareth Jones and Paul Loveridge.

We never saw each other outside of school - we lived miles apart - but while we were at school we were pretty much inseparable. Breaktimes were spent playing football - two against two, a tennis ball, rush goalies and blazers for goalposts. Or we'd stroll around the school grounds discussing the burning issues of the day, like which was better - Wagon Train or Rawhide? Or who would win in a fight - Flint McCullough or Rowdy Yates?

In my mind's eye the school grounds went on forever and it was certainly possible to wander out of sight of the teachers who were meant to be supervising us during break.

This proved especially useful on one particular occasion.

It was the summer of 1964. The annual exams were imminent. We boys and girls were about to be tested on everything from how to calculate the area of a circle to the nominative, vocative, accusative, genitive, dative, and ablative of the Latin for table. (Mensa, Mensa, Mensam, Mensae, Mensae, Mensa, Mensae, Mensae, Mensas, Mensarum, Mensis, Mensis in case you didn't know).

Phil, Gareth, Paul and I agreed General Science was the exam we were dreading most.

Mr. Swallow - the science master - was strict and had told us this year was going to be particularly challenging. We were on the brink of starting our O Level syllabus - O levels were the GCSEs of their day. 'It's time to get serious, ladies and gentlemen,' he said, smacking his workbench with a length of bunsen burner hose to emphasise his point.

Phil, Gareth, Paul and I looked at each other. 'Do I make myself clear…Stone, Jones, Loveridge and Broome?' said Mr. Swallow. 'Yes sir,' we replied, unconvincingly.

Then we had a stroke of luck.

Packing up at the end of the period Paul noticed something in the lab's wastepaper bin. He walked over to the bin under the pretext of throwing something away and instantly realised what he'd spotted was a stencil of an exam paper. (Long before photocopiers and desktop printers, stencils were used to duplicate anything from office memos to church bulletins, not to mention school exam papers).

With old Swallow distracted by one of the swots asking about the difference between a compound and a mixture, Paul carefully lifted the stencil out of the bin and stashed it in his satchel. Phil, Gareth and I looked on, not quite sure what was happening, but a discreet thumbs up from Paul suggested he'd have some good news for us later.

At lunchtime break, the four of us met up on the far side of the playing fields, well away from the teachers' prying eyes. Paul gently removed the stencil from his satchel 'This, my friends,' he said. 'is our guarantee of top marks in next month's science exam'.

We looked more closely at the flimsy piece of blue black paper and sure enough there, beneath the heading *General Science - Form 3,* we could just make out a load of questions. They'd take some deciphering - this was the stencil of the exam paper, the thing that ink was forced through to print the actual paper - but with a bit of work we were sure we'd be able to read them. Once we knew the questions, it would be a simple matter of looking up the answers and memorising them in advance of the exam.

That was when the ill wind of fate delivered a cruel blow.

A sudden breeze snatched up the stencil and wrapped it around Gareth's face. It stuck there just long enough to leave its inky mark and then off it went, spiralling and swooping across the playing fields like some giant, typewritten butterfly. We gave chase but the stencil climbed higher and higher until eventually it got caught in the branches of a tree. It was out of reach. Just like our dreams of getting top marks in that science exam.

Our efforts to cheat were never exposed, though Gareth's blue stained face did lead to some awkward questions. He said it was an allergic reaction to the chlorine in the school's swimming pool. When someone pointed out we hadn't had a swimming lesson for over a week, Gareth scratched madly a his face. 'I think it may be catching,' he'd say, with a wild-eyed stare. That usually brought the conversation to an end. Nobody wanted the *lurgy*.

Remember the dreaded *lurgy*? If you were infected, you could pass it on simply by touching another kid. As soon as you did pass it on you were cured, which was also your cue to give yourself an imaginary injection in the arm which meant you couldn't get the *lurgy* back.

On the subject of the school swimming pool, it's one of my not so fond memories of Sexey's.

After years of fund-raising, planning, excavating and building, the pool had finally opened amid much ceremony and fanfare. At the time it was a state-of-the-art facility. Everyone was hugely excited. Everyone except me. I hated it.

Despite growing up by the sea - well, the liquid mud of the Bristol Channel to be more precise - I'd never learned to swim. On top of that, the school's new pool was outdoors and unheated. It was surrounded by a willow fence, but that did little or nothing to keep the temperature above freezing or repel the biting wind that, even in summer, whipped across the Levels.

Swimming lessons became the stuff of my worst nightmares.

Phil, Gareth, Paul and pretty much everyone else splashed about playfully and swam endless lengths, switching from breast stroke to crawl in the blink of a watery eye. Meanwhile I floundered in the shallow end, barely daring to let go of the side. I shook and I shivered and I clung to my polystyrene float as if my life depended on it, which it might have done had I strayed out of my depth. The only company I had was Robert Callow who, minus his glasses. myopically bumped into anyone who swam within range.

Generally, I was not the sportiest of boys. I scraped into the Under 13's football team. This wasn't because I'd honed any skills during the breaktime kickabouts with Phil and the others, but because I was tall for my age and, as a left back, I could intimidate advancing centre forwards simply by my physical, albeit gangly, presence.

I was OK at cricket until we stopped playing with a soft ball and started playing with a proper cricket ball. As hard as a rock, it was all too easy to imagine the damage it could do and the pain it could cause if it hit you. Fired at you by the bowler or propelled in your direction by the batsman, it was potentially a weapon of mass destruction and when mine was the mass in danger of being destroyed, my response was less 'Owzat!' and more 'Wotthefuck!'

I didn't like gym either.

My mother was risk averse and maybe I inherited some of her fearfulness. Confronted by wall bars and climbing ropes and vaulting horses, I immediately saw the danger. A slip here, a fall there, a sudden loss of balance and who knew what bones you'd break.

So generally I pottered about the gymnasium. I toyed with medicine balls and played around with skipping ropes. I hung from the pull-up beam and did press-ups on the coconut matting - usually no more than two or three before my skinny little arms buckled and gave up the ghost. I moved from one piece of equipment to another, pretending to work out. I was a busy fool doing just enough to avoid the PE teacher's attention. Eventually the bell would toll, signalling the end of another week's torture.

Athletics wasn't much better. My height meant I was able achieve a passable standard in the long jump and the high jump. And my long legs carried me speedily enough over 100 and 220 yards, but any further - the 440, the 880 or, God forbid, the mile - and I struggled, breathless and bent double with stitch by the end.

Then there was the javelin, the discus and the shot put. If ever there was an accident waiting to happen, the javelin, the discus and the shot put was it. Basically it was kids sent to a remote corner of the playing fields, unsupervised and armed with spears, metal rimmed discs and cannon balls. We'd hurl the javelins at each other and see how close we could get without actually mortally wounding anyone. We'd throw a discus up in the air and see if we could hit it with a javelin. We'd play catch with the shots. Or marbles. Or, with an almighty, two-handed downward thrust, we'd see how far we could sink a shot into the ground, digging it out with the sharp end of a javelin after each attempt. None of it had anything to do with the Olympic motto of 'Faster, Higher, Stronger', but it was funnier; definitely funnier than trying to run 100 yards in less than 15 seconds.

CHAPTER 9

HAND SHANDIES & HAND-ME-DOWNS

Chris Costelloe and Dobbs may have been consigned to the dustbin of rubbish names, but I hadn't given up on the potential of a good *nom de guerre*. And *t*he opportunity to fire up my imagination once more came at Sexey's when Gareth Jones and I spotted a girl, Jayne C, cheating in a school exam.

At break, Gareth and I discussed what we'd both seen and what, if anything, we should do about it. We didn't want to snitch on Jayne - nobody likes a snitch - but we knew that somehow the knowledge of her misdemeanour gave us power. 'But what power?' asked Gareth. 'The power of hoodoo,' I suggested. Gareth was in no mood to joke. 'This is serious,' he said sharply. In silence we carried on thinking. Then, 'I know! We could make a couple of bob. We can blackmail her!' said Gareth. Of course! We could threaten to expose Jayne unless she coughed up some cash.

Our dastardly plan took shape over a school dinner of deep fried spam fritters and grey mashed potato followed by tapioca and raspberry jam.

Gareth and I were among the first to arrive in class each morning, so it would be easy to put a note in Jayne's desk without anyone seeing us. We'd hint at what we knew and demand money in return for our silence. We wrote the note - 'We know what you did in the Geog. exam. Leave two shillings in the empty desk at the back of Room 11 by tomorrow morning or we tell. You have been warned. Signed....'

And that was the tricky part. Signed by who?

Obviously we couldn't use our own names. We might have been new to the world of demanding money with menaces but even we knew that using our real names would be, quite literally, a schoolboy error. No, we needed a false name. But not just any old name like Nigel or Clive.

We needed a name that would strike fear into the heart of Jayne; a name that would let her know the blackmailer was serious; a name that sounded so threatening she'd willingly hand over a couple of bob to buy his silence.

For several minutes we wracked our tiny brains, then it came to me like a bolt out of the blue - Black Olonzo, The Red Handed Avenger. I suggested it to Gareth. He rolled it slowly around his tongue a couple of times to test it for menace. 'Black…Olonzo… the Red…Handed…Avenger. Black…Olonzo…the Red… Handed...Avenger.'

Finally he nodded. Black Olonzo, the Red Handed Avenger it was.

As an alias it proved to be about as successful as Dobbs.

No money was forthcoming, the next day or any other day. Not a penny. The whole plot was a complete and utter failure. I was glad really. I had a soft spot for Jayne and in fact she and I went on to win a Smiths Crisps Twist competition at the third year Xmas party.

Flushed with success and overcome by the bond I felt we'd forged on the dance floor, I almost confessed everything and revealed myself as Black Olonzo. But before I could, another Chubby Checker song had kicked in. It was time to twist again and, perhaps for the best, the moment of truth was lost.

My feelings for Jayne were, I guess, the beginning of the boy becoming a man. I was starting to notice girls more and more. *Buffers* Wilkins, for example, a preternaturally well-developed 13 year old whose nickname needs no explanation, and another older girl who I will refer to as CB.

After a trio of my friends and I had watched, wide-eyed and giggling, as she was *titted up* behind the school's woodpile by a fifth former called Eddie, CB became the object of my boyhood fantasies - fantasies which, at the time, I had no idea what to do with. That would come later, after a summer holiday spent sharing a room with a cousin who shall remain nameless.

Night after night, under his bed sheets, my cousin masturbated into his handkerchief, regaling me as he did so with the delights of what he called a *hand shandy*. It sounded like fun and when, a year or so later, I discovered its pleasures - accompanied by mental images of the raven-haired CB and her pneumatic bust - it did indeed prove to be great fun.

My cousin, by the way, was meticulous in his post-ejaculation ritual. Job done, he'd stumble and fumble his way to the bedroom sink and rinse out his hankie before carefully laying it out on the window sill to dry. In the morning he'd fold his hankie neatly and place it in his trouser pocket, where it stayed until his next date with *Five Fingered Mary*.

I still have a copy of my old Sexey's school photograph and there's CB standing at a slight angle to all the other girls, conspicuous by the perfectly formed and obviously firm breasts beneath her shimmering white blouse; breasts of which she was evidently and justifiably proud. I saw a picture of the grown-up CB on Facebook many years later. She was dressed as a belly dancer and I'm happy to report those breasts have definitely stood the test of time.

As well as CB, I also had a bit of a crush on Margaret. She was in my year and backcombed her auburn hair just enough to suggest there was a slightly racy side to her otherwise sweet and innocent appearance. She and her friend often sat in the desks in front of me and my friend, Phil, and I'd occasionally ping her bra strap (looking back, my idea of courtship left a lot to be desired).

To impress her, when we played hangman in free periods I'd test Margaret and her mate with the names of obscure blues singers – Leadbelly, Blind Lemon Jefferson, Big Bill Broonzy. I got the names from leaflets I'd picked up in a local record shop and they were as meaningless and obscure to me as they were to the two girls.

Needless to say, they never guessed them before the hangman's gibbet and its victim were completed. I'd reveal the answer with a smug look on my face and the girls would just look at me with a mixture of pity, boredom and dismay.

It was the kind of showing off that adolescent boys think is seductive but which is actually really rather annoying. A bit like hoping to impress the opposite sex by telling them that a sneeze sends snot flying out of your nose at 100 miles per hour or that in their lifetime the average person produces enough spit to fill two swimming pools.

Around about this time Dad had decided a life on the road was not for him. After years as a reluctant sales rep, he'd finally stumbled across his true vocation - he'd found a way to make a living out of considering others. The 'others' in this instance being the bored and disaffected teenagers of Burnham-on-Sea and the surrounding area.

He'd become a youth leader - at first voluntarily but subsequently, after a year at Westhill Teacher Training College, salaried by the local authority. And, whatever else he may not have been - loving husband, thoughtful father - he was a very good youth leader.

He started a club which he built up from a few kids meeting over frothy coffee in a room above the Silver Lining Cafe to somewhere with its own purpose-built premises and a membership in the hundreds. Along the way he used his gift of the gab to blag everything from temporary premises to fixtures and fittings, not to mention funds.

And the Bay Club (the name coined by my father because Burnham's in a bay and it was a club for the Burnham Area Youth) was a happening place. It was home to practicing pop groups; football, cricket and athletics teams; motorcycle maintenance classes and art classes; snooker players, darts players, table tennis players, would-be boxers, am-dram groups and debating societies.

And once a year when the carnival came to Burnham, the club took charge of decorating the town from top to bottom.

There were giant papier-mâché masks and heads. And enormous pom-poms. There was brilliantly coloured bunting strewn across every street on the procession route and three dimensional hangings on every lamp-post. And every last item was designed by dad and made by club members from whatever he could beg, steal or borrow.

The club also entered a float into the carnival. St.Trinian's is a theme that seems to have stuck in my memory, with dad as the school's headmaster, complete with mortar board, gown and cane, and the club's male and female members dressed up as schoolgirls, complete with short skirts, stockings and suspenders. It was all perfectly harmless fun but decades later, seen through the eyes of a world rightly shocked by revelations about sexual predators like Jimmy Savile, some of the photographs make slightly uncomfortable viewing.

In addition to the decorations and the float, the Bay Club provided the carnival with an army of collectors.

Although officially too young to be a Bay Club member, I was the leader's son, so entitled to the odd privilege and, at carnival time, that included dressing up and rattling a collection tin.

Turning out as a schoolgirl dressed in suspenders and a gym slip didn't really appeal, so I went for something a little less challenging. I dressed up as a Swiss mountaineer. Why a Swiss mountaineer you may ask? Well, it enabled me to finally put to good use the *lederhosen* I had inherited from a German friend of my father.

To cut a long story short, Hans Ledermann ran a herbal pet food company. Dad had worked as one of his sales rep and the two struck up a friendship.

Our families regularly visited each other - Hans and his wife, Trudel (*Uncle Hans* and *Auntie Trudel* - remember the days when friends of your parents became unofficial uncles and aunts?) had a son and a daughter a year or so older than Katina not Katrina and me.

The Ledermanns were comfortably off and now and again their children's hand-me-downs came our way. The blue, hound's-tooth check sports jacket I happily accepted. And the bottle green, crew neck sweater. But the *lederhosen* I was less sure about. Not so dear old dad. Remember he was a bit of a character? Having his freckle faced, red headed, little Leezy Boy dressed up in traditional, hand embroidered, German leather shorts was right up his *strasse*.

He managed to get me to wear them once. To the beach of all places.

Not surprisingly I was the only 12 year old, not just on Berrow Sands but possibly in the entire West of England, who looked like a walking advertisement for the Hitler Youth. The war may have been over for almost 20 years but I could still sense some animosity as I shuffled self-consciously past little clusters of holidaymakers, the mums and dads quickly gathering in their children to protect them from the nasty Nazi boy. I was reminded of the Smitchds.

I vowed never to wear the *lederhosen* again.

That is until carnival came along and I needed a costume. They were quietly going mouldy at the back of my clothes cupboard. I hoiked them out, teamed them with a Tyrollean hat fashioned from an old trilby and accessorised them with a pick axe made from an upturned coat hanger. I had a Swiss mountaineer's outfit quicker than you can say 'yodel-ay-hee-hoo'. For the record, I stuck with the international theme the following year wearing a stripey headscarf and an old silk dressing gown tied at the waist with a length of rope. The finishing touch was a bottle of milk which dangled from my belt. I was a *Milk Sheikh*.

Anyway, back to the Bay Club. As well as the setting for myriad activities, it was a bolt hole for pretty much any teen to twenty-something, 'regardless of race, colour or creed'. Given that everyone in Burnham, with the exception perhaps of Dawn Burke, was Anglo Saxon, white and Christian, this was a noble but utterly pointless clause written into the club's manifesto by dad.

It was a refuge for anyone who just wanted to hang out over a bottle of Coke and a Kit-Kat and chew the fat while the latest hits were being blared out by the jukebox. The jukebox. It became dear old dad's nemesis. In those days it was one play for sixpence (2 1/2p); three for a shilling (5p). What dad could never workout was why, after a night of non-stop music, there was only ever one 146 sixpenny bit in the cash drawer.

He tried everything, from indelible inks to padlocks and chains to try and outwit the kids who he knew were somehow fiddling the machine. He even tried different makes and models of jukebox. It was a battle of wits played out against a soundtrack of Elvis Presley, Cliff Richard, Dion and Del Shannon. And, despite dad's best efforts, a battle he never won.

Aided and abetted by two ladies - the heroic Mrs. South and indomitable Mrs. Howard - dad ran the club 5 nights a week, dealing with everything from hormonal teenage girls looking for a shoulder to cry on to testosterone-fuelled tearaways spoiling for a fight. Lifelong friendships were forged. Romances blossomed. Grudges were forgiven, if perhaps not forgotten. Ever the pacifist, there was never any trouble that dad couldn't deal with. He never raised his fists. Or his voice.

And to this day it's still possible to visit Burnham and find some pensioner sitting on a park bench who will tell you Gordon Broome made them the man (or woman) they are today with his little chats about wars ceasing when men refuse to fight or happiness being like a perfume - *You can't pour it on yourself without getting a few drops on others.*

But even though the club was a huge success and my father's reputation as the saviour of Somerset's wayward youth was growing by the week, we were moving away.

My sister, Katina not Katrina, had become an unmarried mother and that was a bit too characterful even for my dad. I never knew whether he felt ashamed or just plain stupid. Some of his values were oddly Victorian. On occasions, so was his language. He spoke of young women being 'deflowered' by 'filthy rotten swines' and maybe the embarrassment of knowing his own daughter had suffered such a fate was all too much for him.

Whatever his reasoning, Dad decided we should leave Somerset, the Nibletts, the Gibletts and all and move to the Isle of Wight.

I wasn't happy.

Unlike my sister, Katina not Katrina, who by the time she was six had lived in a succession of houses, cottages, tents and caravans and lodged with grandparents, uncles and aunts, I'd only ever known one home. And I liked it. I also liked my friends, my school, my life. Dad tried selling the move to me as an adventure. 'We're moving to an island,' he said. 'Imagine that...an *island*'. He emphasised the word, trying to add a sense of wonder. I presume he hoped my mind's eye would conjure up pictures of almond-eyed maidens hanging garlands around my neck as I stepped off the ferry. He hoped I'd imagine white sands fringed with palm trees and lapped by softly foaming turquoise waves. He hoped I'd see myself snoozing in a hammock, my man Friday gently fanning me while I sipped freshly squeezed papaya juice from a coconut shell.

I didn't know much about the Isle of Wight but I did know it wasn't some exotic, island paradise. How could it be when its self-proclaimed Seven Wonders included *Ryde where you walk* and *Cowes you can't milk*?

Mum and dad said I could stay in Somerset and board at Sexey's if I really didn't want to go with them. I briefly entertained the idea then remembered the horror stories I'd heard from a couple of boarders in my year at school - the nights spent wide awake and dreading the next prank; the cold showers; the breakfasts, dinners and evening meals that somehow all tasted the same; the weekends when the sixth form boarders whiled away the hours with a bit of casual bullying.

No, I decided to take my chances on the Isle of Wight.

CHAPTER 10

CLEAN ROUND THE BEND

In the summer of 1964, with a home-made trailer hitched to the back of the Ford Zephyr Mark 1 convertible off we went, the wind in our hair, Butch the cat in a cardboard box and, in a basket on my mother's lap, Buttons, or Boo Boo for short, the family's peekypoo - a cross between a pekingese and a poodle.

I never saw the Munts, the Chicks, the Nibletts or the Gibletts again. Many years later I heard that the eldest Niblett, Janner, could be found propping up the bar of the Berrow Inn proclaiming loudly, to anyone who'd listen, 'I was a bugger I was'.

I'm not sure that he was.

Though I can still see him, riding a 650cc motorbike with Skip, another of our dogs, flying along at his side. Almost parallel to the tarmac, with all four legs off the ground, Skip's teeth would be firmly buried in Janner's right leg. I guess anyone who can pull that off on a daily basis is entitled to say they were a bugger.

Thinking about it, I did briefly see Robert Niblett again. At the time I'd been away from Berrow for about 15 years, living in London for seven or eight of them. I'd returned for a trip down memory lane and bumped into Rob outside the British Legion club. He said he wasn't surprised to see me back. 'It's a hard place to leave,' he said. 'It gets under your skin'.

He told me he'd tried to escape, upped sticks and moved.

'Where did you go?' I asked. 'Bristol? Birmingham? London? Up north? Down south? Somewhere abroad?'

'Burnham,' he answered (actually less than 10 minutes away on the No. 93 bus).

Anyway, he'd soon got homesick and moved back to Berrow.

Our dog, Skip, incidentally, was a cross between a golden retriever and a labrador and displayed the unconditional love and affection of both breeds (Janner Niblett roaring past on his motorcycle aside). Set free to roam the village where we lived, he often struck up friendships with other families, even taking up residence for a few days here, there and wherever he got the most food and the most fuss made of him.

In other words, Skip was a kind of communal dog.

So it wasn't unusual for boys and girls to turn up on our doorstep and ask if they could borrow him for a couple of hours, take him for a walk, maybe even have him as a houseguest for a while.

And so it was one sunny afternoon that my mother was greeted at the kitchen window by two young boys who were looking for Skip. With a shake of her head mum explained to the boys that Skip would not be coming out to play today. He was on heat and had disgraced himself by chasing the ladies. As punishment, she said, he was tied up round the back.

With a slightly perplexed, not to say panicked look the boys backed away from the window and left.

It emerged some days later that the boys were in fact scouts from one of the troops who regularly camped up the road from us during the summer. They frequented the tea room my parents occasionally ran from our home. The *Skip* they were looking for was not the sex-crazed womaniser imprisoned in our back garden. It was actually *Skip* their scout leader.

So where was I? Oh yes, the Isle of Wight.

Dad had got a job as a youth leader in Sandown, which is where I enrolled at my new school. My new blazer was still to be delivered, so for a while I had to wear my old one.

Not surprisingly, my Sexey's School badge proved to be a source of great amusement.

It's amazing how quickly word got round.

We were only minutes into the first break on my first day and already kids aged from 11 to 18 were coming up to me, pointing at the area around my left breast and sniggering. Girls, in particular, looked at the badge, looked at me then walked away shaking their heads, leaving me crimson-faced with their mocking cat calls of 'Ooh, hello sexy.' still ringing in my ears.

Then there was the matter of my surname. The best nickname my old school chums in Somerset could manage was Broomer. (Interestingly, I was Broomer, my mate Phillip Stone was Stoner but someone else I met from Somerset years later, Mark Windsor, was nicknamed Winds. I'm sure there's a twisted, schoolboy logic in there somewhere).

Anyway, Broomer was just too unimaginative for my new Isle of Wight classmates. They wanted to be a bit more creative. But only a bit. So Broome was briefly Brush before becoming Bog Brush, because he's 'Clean round the bend' as one playground wit explained, warming to the theme and adding to my humiliation.

I tried not dignify my new name with a response whenever possible, asking everyone to call me Leo instead. I figured it sounded marginally more manly than Leon, which I had convinced myself sounded like a ballet dancer or a hairdresser, neither of which I wanted to sound like.

And as for where we lived, once again the gods of comedy names had conspired to make my life difficult. Not for the family Broome a house in Brading or Bembridge or Shanklin. Oh no.

That would have been too easy. No, we took up residence in Queen Bower. It was only three miles from where I went to school but nobody had heard of it. 'Sorry? Did you say queers' bowels?' asked my interrogators.

'No', I protested, 'I live in...look, it's near Apse Heath'.

'Chaps' teeth? Are you saying you like chaps' teeth? Are you a homo? Leon's definitely a homo's name'.

As a play on words goes, none of it was very sophisticated. It barely made sense. But that didn't seem to trouble the tormentors who guffawed like hyenas at their puny punning and my embarrassment.

Salvation, in part, came quite unexpectedly.

For a while, after school finished I met dad at his office and cadged a lift home in the latest of his dropheads - a fire engine red Triumph Herald Vitesse. But the day finally came when I had to face the ordeal of the school bus. Pointed in the direction of the right bus by a helpful prefect, I got on board and climbed the stairs to the top deck (we were segregated - boys on top, girls down below). I tried not to look lost and helpless. I tried not to look like the newbie, Leon Broome, aka Brush, Bog Brush, the sexy schoolboy with a fondness for queers' bowels and chaps' teeth.

I stopped halfway down the bus next to a kid in short trousers - a first former I guessed. I nodded at the empty seat next to him. He immediately turned his face to the window, steamed up the glass with his breath and drew the classic - cock and balls. I don' t know if it was directed at me or just something he did, but I sat down anyway.

The bus pulled away and we were only minutes into the journey when it hit me - I had no idea how or where I was going to get off. Should I ring the bell when I thought I was near home?

Or was there a designated stop where the bus would just come to a halt? Ringing the bell might confuse things. In the secret code of bus drivers it might be the signal to drive on - no passengers alighting. I had vague recollections of bus journeys in the past when one ring seemed to mean stop and two rings meant don't stop. Or was it the other way round? And that was in Somerset.

They probably did things differently here.

Maybe I should just go downstairs, stand nonchalantly on the open platform at the back of the bus and wait for the driver to see me and stop. It was getting dark. I wasn't even sure I'd recognise the turning for Queen Bower anyway.

There was no conductor or teacher on board to turn to. And it was one of those old style buses with the driver closeted in a cab at the front. I thought about asking the inkie next to me for help, but he was completely lost in his own little world, drawing an intricate cock and balls on the inside back cover of his English Literature exercise book. At least now I knew it was a hobby and nothing personal.

Then, just up ahead, I spotted a phone box that I thought was quite close to where I lived.

I looked around hoping someone else would make the first move. Surely I wasn't the only person getting off at my stop. Then I remembered the blank looks I'd got whenever I'd mentioned I lived in Queen Bower. I was clearly on my own.

I decided against ringing the bell, opting instead to go downstairs, hang about at the back of the bus and hope it stopped. As soon as it did, I'd casually step off and take leave of my fellow passengers.

And hang about I did. And hang about. And hang about.

The phone box flashed by. A village that I'd never heard of came and went, welcoming careful drivers then thanking them for driving carefully. The bus showed no signs of slowing down.

For what seemed like an eternity I stood there, convinced every girl on the lower deck was looking at me, wondering what on earth the newbie, Leon Broome, aka Brush, Bog Brush, the sexy schoolboy with a fondness for queers' bowels and chaps' teeth was doing.

There was nothing else for it. Wherever we were, this was my stop.

I don't know if you've ever seen someone step off the back of a double-decker bus doing 40 miles an hour along an unlit country lane. But to anyone who might have been watching, it must have looked like a magic trick. Now you see him. Now you don't. I went head over heels. I went arse over tit. Basically anything that could go over anything else did.

I ended up in a crumpled heap at the side of the road. In the dark, in the rain and with the rear lights of the bus a fast fading glow in the pitch black.

My knees were torn to shreds. The skin on my hands was scraped off almost through to the bone. Not only was I bloodied and bruised, I'd missed my stop by at least two miles and faced a long, wet and painful walk home. I think I may have burst into tears when I finally made it.

But every cloud has a silver lining. I had a couple of days off school while my wounds healed (they were of course mental as well as physical - oh the embarrassment of stepping off that speeding bus) and by the time I went back I had my new blazer, so at least there was no more Sexey's School badge.

My new school badge bore the motto *Endure & Conquer*. However, I decided I would not be enduring or attempting to conquer the journey by school bus ever again. From now on I would be cycling to school and back.

A few months later we moved out of Queen Bower and into the sensibly named village of Adgestone. Another problem solved. All I had to deal with now was the Leon, Leo, Broome, Brush, Bog Brush thing.

Now all of this may sound like I was the centre of attention at my new school with hordes of kids queueing up, if not to admire me at least to ridicule me, my Sexey's school badge, my name, my address. OK, I was being talked about and, as Oscar Wilde said, that's better than not being talked about.

But, despite everything, my appeal, even as a figure of fun, was partially overshadowed by the arrival of another boy who started on exactly the same day as me. He was as loud as I was quiet. Down from London, he was a city slicker to my country bumpkin. He was an Artful Dodger to my Oliver. He swaggered where I shuffled. He was loose limbed, all elbows and *Knees Up Mother Brown*. I was hands in pockets, shoulders hunched.

Dropping aitches left, right and centre, he spoke thirteen to the dozen while I struggled to get a word in edge ways. While he impressed with his claims to know Van Morrison's band, Them, the closest connection I had with showbiz was a cousin who'd gone to the same school as one of The Applejacks (who?).

He drew adoring crowds with his piano playing in the school hall at break and he also had a little finger that was scarred and slightly bent. Essentially it was disfigured, but still it seemed to make him even more alluring to the girls of 4B.

His name was Geoff. We were bound by our newness and, as much as he annoyed me, I guess I kind of clung to him in those early days, hoping some of his brash confidence would rub off on me. It didn't. But something better happened.

CHAPTER 11

FIRST LOVE

While we were living in Apse Heath, I had started admiring from afar a girl called Susan. She didn't go to my school but lived up the road, and my plan was a kind of courtship by osmosis. So I hung about in the lane near her house hoping our eyes would meet as she walked to the village shop or flashed by in her brother's car.

I would spend hours just waiting for the fleeting moment when I saw her. I never actually spoke to her (difficult from 200 yards away or through the windscreen of a speeding Morris Minor) but I was convinced that somehow she'd eventually read my mind. She'd run towards me in slow motion, her tumbling and tousled blonde locks lustrous in the summer sunshine. She'd throw herself into my open arms, her rosebud lips pursed in readiness for the kiss that would seal our undying love. After a long, lingering embrace, she'd climb on to the crossbar of my bike and we'd cycle off into the sunset. We'd be happy ever after.

Of course it never happened.

The closest I got was when her mate came up to me and said 'My friend fancies you'. It wasn't exactly the greatest declaration of love everlasting that I'd ever heard, but it was encouragement enough to keep me hanging about in that lane for a few more weeks.

And it was during one such vigil that I met Jelly, or Martin to give him his proper name.

I recognised him from school. He was, to be blunt, overweight. Not obese by any means, but a bit on the wobbly side, hence Jelly. Anyway, he was out walking Bitey, his half blind dog (by that I mean the dog was partially sighted, not a cross between a blind dog and some other breed).

He stopped to say hi and we got talking. I can't really remember what we talked about, but it was the beginning of a friendship that would last for many years. Just as important, it was my introduction into Jelly's circle of friends. And, without a malevolent bone in his body, he was a popular kid.

Before I knew it I was mates with Wacko, Mitch, Titch, Baxter and Dickie, with Mac, Mick, Knobby, Cabbage and Danny, to name but a few.

And, much to my delight, everyone agreed Geoff was an arse. It was time to move on and out of his shadow.

I soon became one of the gang. I joshed with my newfound pals. I bantered with them in the school corridors as we moved between classrooms. We gave each other dead legs and playful punches on the arm. We hung out in *the bogs* discussing Judy B's fabulous tits and the rumour that a bust developing cream had turned them bright blue.

I appealed to my new best friends' better nature and they stopped calling me Brush. I was now Leo, at least to anyone who mattered. And, as my confidence grew, my shy charm even started working on some of the girls. Geoff meanwhile was losing his allure as slowly but surely the girls began to realise that there was more to life than a deformed pinkie and a vamped piano version of *Baby Please Don't Go*.

It had taken a while. For weeks, maybe months, I'd drifted about trying to look enigmatic but succeeding only in looking sad. In desperation I'd latched on to the nerds and the geeks. Often desperate themselves, they'll talk to anyone and I surprised even myself with how much I knew about stamp collecting. Was it really me I could hear saying 'Yes, I believe that Nyasaland £25 stamp first appeared in 1895'?

But, thanks to Jelly, all that was behind me. Now I had proper friends. Cool friends. And friends of friends.

And on Saturday nights we all met up at the 69 Club. We arrived from all four corners of the Island on special double decker buses laid on by the club's organisers.

Disgorged at the Pavillion, the Royal York, the Manor House or the Oasis in Ryde - the club was something of a moveable feast - we'd show our 69 Club membership cards, pay our 2/6d, nod coolly to the bouncers and make our entrance, usually to a warm-up soundtrack supplied by DJ, 'I Am, I Am The Mighty Ruler' Spike.

A couple of light ales later and it was time to strut our stuff.

In made-to-measure suits from Hepworths, in parallel trousers and waisted jackets with either two 7" side vents or a single 14" centre vent, (there was presumably some unwritten law that said the total *ventage* had to add up to 14"), in tab collar shirts and knitted ties, we danced, shimmied and whirled like diabolos, usually near rather than with girls wearing shift dresses and slingback shoes in shades of baby blue and powder pink.

We did the Shake, the Hitchhiker and the Mashed Potato to sounds of the swinging '60s cranked out by the 69 Club's legendary house band, The Cherokees, who played note perfect covers of everyone from The Beatles and The Rolling Stones to Otis Redding, The Four Tops and The Temptations.

In a weekly ritual, we all held hands, (if you were lucky you got a girl on one side at least), formed a massive circle and wave after wave charged into the centre, crashing into each other while The Cherokees roared their way through Chuck Berry's *Anthony Boy*.

In between songs, members of the band read out messages given to them by people in the crowd. *Tell Dave I fancy him - Linda*; *Pete - Rob says mine's a light and bitter*; *Brush likes queers' bowels*. (I hadn't completely left my past behind).

I took the opportunity to have some announcements of my own read out. They were messages promoting my new band. The band didn't actually exist but they had a name - another pseudonym that I was convinced would lead to fame and fortune.

The announcements were meant to be the start of a whispering campaign that would get people clamouring to see and hear more from the mysterious band. Initially I wanted to protect my anonymity in all of this, so I persuaded a slightly inebriated Dickie Donn to pass on *hot off the press* stories for The Cherokees to read out.

And so, for several weeks, the PA crackled with news of Dernie Ernie and The Cornflake Men, their forthcoming tour and their debut single, *Tweedledeedee and Tweedledeedum.*

The plan was, in the face of overwhelming public demand, I would finally reveal myself. (I'd worry about who the Cornflake Men were at some other time). I'd be an overnight sensation. I'd leave school, marry '60s dolly bird, Cathy McGowan, and live in a penthouse apartment overlooking Carnaby Street.

Unfortunately, like Chris Costelloe, Dobbs and Black Olonzo before him, Dernie Ernie proved to be another damp squib. I quietly disbanded the band.

I still had disc jockey Jonathan Sundae up my sleeve, not to mention *Smile*, his theme tune - *Just because my teeth are pearly. Just because my hair is curly. Just because I always wear a smile.*

But I was beginning to wonder if this whole name change thing really was my passport to stardom.

As it happens, I did form a real band some years later and, of course, the question of a name was agonised over by myself and co-founder, Johnny Bull. We dismissed Captain Brassbound's Feathered Baghdad Scissors (the result of a cut and paste exercise at school a few years earlier), thought about Garbage, Greasegun & Lunchpack, mulled over Alec Smart and the GCEs, before finally settling on Waiter My Bill.

As well as featuring on fly posters - *Thrill to Waiter My Bill. What? Another gleaming semipro band gettinitogevvah?* - the name appeared briefly in the classified ads in the back pages of Melody Maker.

It was part of a deal we struck with the landlord of the Pied Bull in London's Islington in order to secure a Sunday night residency. And it very nearly lured the late, great John Peel to one of our gigs.

In his regular column in Sounds - another popular music paper of the time - the influential radio presenter, record producer and journalist said that on occasions he would go and check out new acts purely on the strength of their name.

This particular week, he wrote, he'd wanted to go and see Waiter My Bill, but unable to find them listed anywhere he'd gone instead to watch a band called Bontemps Roulez.

Renowned for championing unknown bands, imagine what might have been had Peely turned up at the Pied Bull and heard us grinding our way through *Comfy Mattress* or *Can't Play Guitar.*

As it was, he didn't.

Personally I blamed the fact that our residency went from a packed house to no punters at all in precisely three weeks on that single twist of fate and not on the fact that sometimes, to be frank, Waiter My Bill couldn't carry a tune in a bucket.

CHAPTER 12

THE OH BE JOYFULS

I met Christine, the girl who would eventually become my first wife, at the 69 Club, Ryde Pavilion, sometime in 1966. I say 'met' but I already knew her from school. Like me and Geoff, she was what the locals called an *overner* - someone newly arrived on the Island. She was another Londoner and shared Geoff's confidence, though in her case it wasn't quite so misplaced.

She was very pretty with a turned up nose. Her dark hair was cropped in a fashionable mod style which was yet to be adopted by the other girls (it was only a 30 minute ferry crossing, but some things took a lot longer to make it over from the mainland). Like her hair, her skirts were short and I remember her navy blue school jumper was stretched over her already quite noticeable bosom. You could say she stood out.

But although she was in my year at school it was unlikely that she noticed me at first.

Like most teenage boys, I was a boy. Like most teenage girls, she was a woman - a fact that had not escaped the attention of one or two older boys, including the visiting pop star who had plucked her from the audience at Ventnor's Winter Gardens so that he could exercise his *droit de singer.*

I didn't know much about the tough acts I had to follow when, emboldened by a sniff of the barmaid's apron and encouraged by the fact that her judgment was clearly blurred by one too many vodka and limes, I went up to Christine at the 69 Club and asked her to dance.

She fell into my arms (that may have had more to do with the vodka and lime than my magnetic charms) and by the following Saturday we were a couple. So, it was pack your bags Peter, ta ta Tim, it's time to move on Malcolm and good riddance Roger, the Big L is moving in.

Apart from a single, snatched kiss with a girl named Janice, until I met Christine my raging hormones had been largely unsatisfied.

So I was determined to make up for lost time. We snogged and gave each other love bites at every opportunity. We fondled and groped each other anywhere and everywhere - in bus shelters and beach huts, in her brother's old car on her parents' driveway, at parties, on park benches and at the back of the bus home from the 69 Club.

Eventually I lost my virginity to Christine. It was at her house. I'd stayed the night - in the spare room of course - and in the morning, while her dad was at work and her mum was out shopping, Christine slipped into the bed beside me. Thankfully she took charge. I was, remember, a virgin. I can't recall exactly what happened or how long it lasted - not very long I imagine - but I do know my first words after it was over were 'Are your pregnant?'

I was clueless.

There was no sex education at school in those days. My parents had told me nothing. The closest I'd come to learning about contraception was overhearing someone in the barbers asking for a packet of the *oh be joyfuls*. I knew they were 3/9d for three. And that was it.

In a blur of post-coital bliss tinged with panic, Christine reassured me that she wouldn't be having our baby any time soon, just as long as I'd withdrawn at the appropriate moment - though I'm not sure her choice of words was quite so clinical.

Anyway, I was pretty sure I had, so that was a relief.

So too was the fact that I'd finally had full on sex. That afternoon, as I walked home across the fields, I admit I felt rather pleased with myself. Leon Broome, aka Brush, Bog Brush, the sexy schoolboy with a fondness for queers' bowels and chaps' teeth, was shagging perhaps the prettiest and possibly the sexiest girl in school.

From that day forward we had sex whenever we could. There was no readily available contraceptive pill in those days and even if I'd known where to buy condoms, and been brave enough to ask for them, I would still probably have preferred to spend my money on the new Beatles album or the latest Jimi Hendrix single.

So our chosen method of birth control remained *coitus interruptus*, which meant that once a month there was the agonising wait for Christine's period.

And there were other repercussions.

On Saturday nights when we didn't go out, Christine and I would babysit for Barry and Carol, the couple who lived across the road from me. As soon as we were on our own and the children were sound asleep, we'd be upstairs on the parents' double bed, going at it like mad.

One night we got a bit careless and the climax of our bout of passion left a damp patch on Barry and Carol's lemon yellow, candlewick bedspread.

After a couple of minutes frozen to the spot and staring in silence at the mark of our guilt, Christine disappeared into the bathroom. She emerged, seconds later, with a fistful of wet toilet paper. She rubbed frantically at the stain. In the disbelieving blink of an eye, it darkened and doubled in size. We looked at each other in horror.

Without saying a word, we both knew what we had to do. Whipping the cover off the bed, we raced downstairs with it. Somehow we'd have to dry it out before Barry and Carol got home.

The washing line was out of the question. It was drizzling outside. And besides the line was clearly visible from my parents' kitchen window. If my mum saw us, apparently hanging out washing, she was bound to come over. She'd tell us off for going above and beyond the call of duty as babysitters. And next time she saw Carol, she'd no doubt tick her off too for taking advantage. In the confused conversation that would inevitably follow, it's highly likely that mum and Carol would eventually put two and two together.

Never mind bedspreads, Christine and I knew that would be curtains for our love life.

We checked out the kitchen. There was no tumble dryer. Which left us with no option other than to dry the bedspread in front of the gas fire. Simple enough. But somehow we must have got distracted (possibly those raging hormones again). Suddenly the room smelt of burning candlewick. We snatched the cover away from the heat.

But it was too late.

We examined the damage. The water mark had dried out alright. In fact it had passed through dry, gone on to super dry before finally arriving at flammable. The site of a small fire had left a scorch mark about 3" in diameter.

We went back upstairs and remade the bed. The layout of the human body being what it is, it didn't matter which way we spread out the cover, the scorch mark stayed resolutely slap bang in the middle. There was nothing we could do. Maybe Barry and

Carol wouldn't notice it. Or if they did, maybe they'd think a flying pig had crapped on their bed.

Anyway, when they came home later that evening we told them everything was fine. We'd watched television and not heard a peep out of the kids. Then we skulked off into the night. The matter was never mentioned. And we were never asked to babysit for Barry and Carol again. Funny that.

Throughout this time my social life, my Saturday nights at the 69 Club, my afternoons spent slurping a Cola Float at the Wimpy Bar in Ryde or sipping a hot blackcurrant at the Paramount Cafe were funded by a summer holiday job. I worked alongside Jelly at his parents' tea room - Vernon Cottage - in Shanklin Old Village.

(The hot blackcurrant, incidentally, was always a shrewd purchase. Unlike tea or coffee, it didn't come pre-cooled by milk. It stayed undrinkably hot for ages, which meant you could linger for longer in the cafe. Asked by the cafe's increasingly impatient proprietor to hurry up and vacate the table, all you could do was point at the still scalding hot mug of blackcurrant. You'd shrug and make a gesture that said you weren't going anywhere in a hurry, except maybe the Burns Unit at the local hospital if he made you down your drink too quickly).

But back to Jelly and Vernon Cottage. After an emergency operation to have his appendix removed, Jelly had shed several stone and, thanks to the kindness of his classmates, was now known by the marginally - but only marginally - less offensive nickname, Tub.

And for two glorious summers Tub and I toiled away satisfying the appetites and quenching the thirsts of holidaymakers who we secretly referred to as 'piles' , because they were red, they hung about in bunches and they were a pain the arse.

We made morning coffee and afternoon tea. We made hot chocolate, Horlicks and Bournvita. We whisked fluorescent milkshakes flavoured with fruit-based powders of dubious origin. We delivered salads and various savouries on toast to families who were either sheltering from the rain or simply starving - the meagre B of their DB&B a distant memory and the D still several, ravenous hours away.

We served rock cakes, scones, jam and cream, all whipped up by Roy, Tub's lovely dad (Brylcreemed hair and bristling moustache) and his delightful mum, Portia (larger than life in more ways than one). He ground his teeth noisily and relentlessly and, from behind the tea urn, growled at any customer who had the temerity to ask 'Is it fresh cream in the fresh cream sponge?' (It wasn't). She busied herself baking mountains of scones, la la la-ing merrily as she covered herself and the kitchen in flour before eventually disappearing off to play bridge or have coffee with *the girls*.

Drifting in and out of this barely organised chaos was Lindy, one of Tub's sisters. She was in her early 20s and the sweetest of girls, but her behaviour could be a bit unpredictable - the result, I think, of a traumatic bang on the head when she was little. I can still picture the perplexed looks on customers' faces when, halfway through their meal, Lindy would appear out of nowhere and silently clear their table.

Washing up, pipe gripped between his toothless gums, was Mr. Lyons. A grizzled old sea dog, he claimed to have hacked the hands off proto-nationalist Chinamen while serving in the British navy during the Boxer Rebellion. He threatened Tub and I with the same fate if we ever emptied the leftover water from the boiled egg pan into his washing up bowl. It would give him warts he told us, with a murderous stare. We never argued.

Nor did we argue with the customer who, parodying Roy's poster that read, *A friendly warning - there are three step down into the garden*, left a postcard on their table saying *A friendly warning - avoid the coffee.*

Having personally sampled the coffee we made using catering packs labelled 'Kompletely Koffee - Real Coffee Taste At A Fraction Of The Cost. Produce of Romania' , it was a perfectly reasonable piece of advice.

During our afternoon break, Tub and I would jump into his mum's gleaming white Sunbeam Rapier convertible (he was a year older than me and, by our second summer of working together, old enough to drive). With the roof down, we'd cruise Shanklin sea front and admire from a car the Swedish au pairs who invaded the town every year between June and September.

I really liked Tub's parents and couldn't believe it when, some years later, Tub took a phone call at my flat to be told his dad had committed suicide. Apparently he'd simply got up that morning, walked down to Shanklin beach and carried on walking...out into the cold, grey sea. Close as we were, I didn't ask Tub about his dad's death, why he thought he did it, if there was a note. It seemed like prying; indelicate and tactless at a time when one of my best ever mates was consumed with grief.

By tragic coincidence, Tub lost his own life at sea, knocked overboard one stormy night while he was working on the boats that supply the North Sea oil rigs. I think about him a lot and wish he were still alive so we could grow old together. He was funny, kind and a good friend.

CHAPTER 13

BREAKING UP IS *BIT EASY* TO DO

Of course, as well as a social life and sex life, I still had a school life. School was OK.

I was the original *Could Try Harder Kid*. The trouble was nobody, especially my parents who were preoccupied with their own dysfunctional lives, seemed to care if I tried harder or not. So I didn't. I scraped together a few O Levels - not enough to get me into the sixth form but not so few that I had to repeat the fifth form. Instead I, and a few other not so bright sparks, ended up in a year known as 6E.

Now, what we were meant to do in 6E was swot up on the O Levels we'd failed so miserably at in the summer and get ready to sit them again in the autumn. While we were doing that we were allowed to begin our A Level studies. The plan being we would pass our O Level retakes which would qualify us to move into the sixth form proper in the new year. And we would become fully fledged sixth formers having already started the A Level coursework whilst studying for the shortfall in our O Levels.

Dreamt up by the school, the plan presumably made sense to somebody. But we all know what can happen to even the best laid plans.

In reality, those of us who weren't quite as dumb as our exam results suggested, worked out that we could bunk off an O Level lesson by telling the teacher we had a clashing A Level lesson we couldn't possibly miss. At the same time could bunk off an A Level lesson by saying to the teacher we had a clashing O Level lesson we couldn't possibly miss.

We relied on our teachers being too busy (or too lazy) to compare timetables, which left us in a lesson-free limbo we could fill in whatever way took our fancy.

Mostly my fancy was hiding out in empty classrooms, sometimes with Judy B. I never found a way to broach the subject of her allegedly blue breasts, though I did spend a lot of time looking at them and wondering. We lost touch after school and she eventually emigrated to Australia. 40 years later we became friends again on Facebook, but I felt the moment to ask about her tits had probably passed.

When I wasn't ducking and diving between vacant classrooms, I was pretending to study in the library but secretly passing lewd notes to the newfound love of my life and generally loafing and laughing, usually in the company of Tub, Dick and two new boys - Johnny Bull and Chris Howe. Johnny was really good at art and used his talents, together with his wit, to enhance the photographs in the library's collection of books on wildlife (particularly the pictures of sea lions). Chris was rumoured to be some sort of Oxbridge-bound boy genius, but he hid his intellectual superiority well and just made me laugh till it hurt. Both Johnny and Chris, along with Dick, Laurence Mitchell and Nick Dorley-Brown, would become lifelong friends and each, in their own way, would inform, influence, educate, amuse and entertain me more than anyone else I ever met.

Apart from our friendship, we merry band, and one or two others like John Baxter (*The Hot Hadleigh Baxendale*, of whom more later) also shared a language which I'll call *Sandonian*. I have no idea how it started or who started it, but I can tell you it was *bit cheap*.

Let me explain.

The vocabulary was based on taking a word then using its opposite to express what you wanted to say. So if something was *hot*, you said it was *cold*. If something was *fast* you said it was *slow*. If someone was *thin* you said they were *fat*. To emphasise your point you could preface your chosen word with either *bit, rather* or *small* - there were no rules on this, it was simply a matter of personal preference - and *bit, rather* or *small* meant *very*.

So, one of the Paramount cafe's piping hot blackcurrant drinks would be described as *bit cold*. A car driving by at speed would be *small slowcoach*. At the time, I would have been described as *rather fat bloke*. (This was a period in life my when, courtesy of Dick Donn, graffiti appeared on the school blackboards imploring people to 'Forget Oxfam and Feed Leo').

Cheap was a catch-all and meant good or excellent, hence *bit cheap* meaning *very good*.

And, somewhat confusingly, *hot* was not always used as the opposite of cold. It could also mean *I don't like that* or *bad*.

There were other standard *Sandonian* words and phrases, like *bother,* meaning *Please don't do that* or *I don't like it.* So if someone was annoying you by kicking the back of your seat at the cinema, you'd turn around and say 'Bother!' *Don't bother,* meanwhile, meant *Yes please, do...absolutely*. So in response to the question 'Can I buy you a drink?' you would reply 'Don't bother'.

In addition to *bit, rather* or *small*, you could give your words or phrases even more emphasis by introducing them with a long draw out *Yessssss* for something negative (remember the rule of opposites) or, of course, a *Noooooo* for a something positive. For example, *Noooooo don't bother to look at bit cheap bird* would translate as *Look at that very attractive young lady over there*.

Any vocal expression was usually accompanied by a facial expression that involved pursing your lips and shaking your head.

Over time the language became even more creative, not to say convoluted. If someone was drunk, in basic *Sandonian* they could be described as *bit sober*. But like all languages *Sandonian* was constantly evolving. So *bit sober* became *Sir Garry Sobers*. In the same way, you might describe a freezing cold day as *Walmington On Sea* or, to really make your point, *Yessssss, bother, bit Walmington On Sea*.

There was even a variation that involved adding *idge* on to the end of words, so, for example, *Sir Garry Sobers* became *Sir Garry Soberidge.*

I don't know whether it was exclusive to our small group, to Sandown Grammar or even to the Isle of Wight, but whenever I meet up with Johnny, Chris, Nick, Laurence and Dick - even though more than 50 years have passed - we invariably exchange a few words in *Sandonian.* At the very least, we OAPs look each other up and down, purse our lips, shake our heads and say 'Bit Jimmy Young'.

Anyway, back to the O Level / A Level scam. It seemed like a *bit cheap idea* at the time, but actually it turned out to be a *rather hot idea.* Avoiding studying for O Levels or A Levels only meant I ultimately achieved nothing of any note in either. In the years since I've tried to console myself with those school of hard knocks, university of life clichés, but to be honest I wish I had actually tried harder.

I clung on at school for as long as I could. Until the day, in fact, when my form-master took me to one side and asked if I'd thought about leaving. 'No, ' I replied. 'Well, perhaps you should,' he said.

Fleetingly, I considered playing my *Get Out Of Jail Free* card.

I'd been diagnosed with *petit mal* epilepsy as a toddler. To eliminate the risk of seizures and further damage to my brain, I'd been prescribed a daily dose of *phenytoin sodium.*

Apparently one of the potential side effects was occasional bouts of sleepiness. I'd been given a letter explaining this to any teacher who might otherwise misinterpret me dozing off during class as laziness or a lack of interest.

I can't say I was actually ever aware of any side effects, but now seemed like a good time to mention my *special needs*. Maybe they'd save me from an early exit. But, even as the subterfuge took shape in my mind, I remembered that I'd been given the all-clear about three years before.

I'd stopped taking the tablets. There was no excuse for my lack of academic achievement other than I couldn't be arsed.

Besides, Tub was off to join the merchant navy as a trainee officer with Shell. My girlfriend was planning to become a student nurse. Wacko had already signed for Southampton as an apprentice professional footballer, Mick had gone into the army. The gang was definitely breaking up. I'd miss Johnny, Chris, Dick, Laurence and Nick, but there seemed little point in flogging a dead horse.

It was the summer of 1967 and my school days were finally over.

I don't remember discussing it with my parents. In truth, I don't think they had much time for anything but their own problems. Their marriage had always been rocky, perhaps cursed from the start by mum's mum, who'd refused to even go to the wedding. And now, my father's wandering eye had found something new to focus on.

Once a year, the youth club he ran played host to something called International Camp. Hundreds of bright young things from France, Germany and Scandinavia descended on dad's little corner of the Isle of Wight.

Billeted in the surrounding school buildings, they went about their entirely wholesome activities - table tennis, bracing country walks, picnics on the playing fields - under the watchful eyes of responsible adults, some of whom, it would be revealed in the Broome household at least, were engaged in slightly less innocent pastimes.

Yes, though in later life he insisted the relationships were never anything more than platonic, International Camp presented my dad with a golden opportunity to indulge his fondness for younger women with foreign accents. (I should point out here that he never did anything illegal, just a little ill-advised perhaps).

His first dalliance was with a German lady. Let's call her Anna.

By the time Anna returned to *Deutschland* dad was smitten.

At home he domiciled himself in the spare bedroom, the better to concentrate on the love letters he and his *fräulein* exchanged. These he wrote (and presumably read) to the tune of *Kumbaya My Lord*, which he played over and over again on a small portable tape recorder he kept by his bedside. It was a particularly miserable version of a particularly miserable song and its monotonous drone crept under the bedroom door and added to the already gloomy atmosphere around the house.

Dad emerged from his self-imposed exile only at meal times and to go to work. Otherwise he was invisible.

We later realised he was often lost in what he and his *liebling* called *TT*. Mum had stumbled across the term in one of Anna's letters to dad.

TT, the letter explained, was *Thinking Time*; a pre-arranged moment during each day when dad and the newfound *platonic* love of of his life would think really hard about each other. The idea was that their thoughts would collide - somewhere over central France I imagine -   and in a kaleidoscope of rainbow colours, in a shower of cupids, stardust, hearts and flowers, dad and his *Deutsche* Anna would instantly be as one. Though separated by hundreds of miles they would be together, in mind if not in body. Typical dad. If he'd just gone for a quick snog now and then he probably wouldn't have been such a tightly wound ball of frustration and conflicted ideals.

Anyway, I forget how long the relationship went on. I do remember being asked by my mother to write a letter to this 'other woman', telling her she was breaking up our happy home. I'm not sure I ever put pen to paper. My heart wasn't really in it. The truth was our home had long since ceased to be happy and anyway, in time the whole thing went away. But there would be other International Camps, other blue eyed blondes speaking broken English to turn dad's head and prick up his ears.

Eventually my mother decided enough was enough.

Our home was breaking up anyway. My sister, Katina not Katrina, had got married and moved away and, despite my somewhat paltry qualifications, I'd managed to get a job on the mainland.

And so it was that one day in November 1967, mum, dad and I walked away from our cottage in Adgestone, got in the car, caught the ferry from Yarmouth to Lymington and prepared to go our separate ways.

CHAPTER 14

ALL EYES ON ME

Obsessed with the romantic notion of returning to my roots and at the same time pursuing a career in advertising, a visit to the Labour Exchange in Sandown on the Isle of Wight and a scroll through their Roladex had revealed a frankly unexpected job opportunity - working in the advertising department of Clarks Shoes in Street, Somerset. It was two birds killed with one stone. At the time I didn't realise that the birds I'd killed were albatrosses.

Mum, meanwhile, was off to help her sister and brother-in-law run the village stores in Bampton, Devon. Dad had offered to deliver mum and I to our new lives, before returning to the Isle of Wight and moving into a one bedroomed flat above a bric-a-brac shop in Shanklin where he'd get on with his old life, courting and cavorting with any eligible foreign female who came his way.

Things did not get off to the best of starts - an omen perhaps for the way things would eventually turn out. We'd barely got off the ferry when an oncoming car veered across our path.

The collision wasn't too bad. Mum bumped something or other and forever after would refer to *The Accident* (and by association my father) as the root cause of every single ache or pain she ever suffered. I was oblivious to the skidding and the screeching and ultimately the collision, lost in thoughts about what the hell I was doing, barely out of short trousers and about to start work a million miles from everyone and everything that was familiar to me. Anyway, with the help of the local constabulary blame was apportioned, insurance details exchanged and finally we resumed our journey.

Our first port of call was my sister's where I was being dropped off before dad took mum on to Devon. Katina not Katrina had moved back to Somerset too and was living with her new husband, Robert, a man she'd met through a lonely hearts column. He'd come down from Scotland, with all his worldly possessions in a small suitcase.

They married in haste - he wore an old sales rep suit thoughtfully sold to him by my father - and they repented at leisure (or least my sister did, but that's another story - her's and not really mine to tell). Anyway, I was going to live with them and Danny, Katina not Katrina's little boy, in a cottage which by coincidence was just a few miles from Clarks and my new job.

That night we all sat down for our last supper together. I couldn't hold back the tears. I guess I was sad and I was scared. I knew that from that moment on there was no family home to return to and no one to support me - dad had made it clear he no longer wanted the responsibilities of parenthood and mum had gone pretty much penniless and cap in hand to live in my Auntie Lorna and Uncle Gordon's spare room. They'd let her take Boo Boo, her precious peekypoo, but any more house guests were out of the question.

121

So, for now at least, this was it.

The cottage was a two up two down on East Street Corner, West Pennard. It would probably be described as 'cosy' now. Then it was just plain pokey. And damp, despite the best efforts of a two bar electric fire. And when the wind was in the right direction (or to be more accurate, the wrong direction) it smelt faintly of bird shit, courtesy of the battery chicken farm just a few yards down the road.

And it was from this cottage, early one gloomy Monday morning in October, that I set out to start my life as a grown-up. I waited on East Street Corner for the works bus to pick me up.

There was a fleet of works buses in those days, gathering up employees from here, there and everywhere, dropping them off in Street then picking them up at the end of the day to take them home. I stood anxiously at the stop. I was beginning to wonder if I'd done the right thing when all of a sudden my bus emerged out of a swirling mist. It juddered to a halt.

There was no turning back now.

The door wheezed open and a fat man in a cap nodded disinterestedly in my direction. I took it as an invitation to get on board. I tried not to catch anyone's eye as I walked down the aisle, eventually finding a seat at the back. A fug of cigarette smoke hung in the air. Everybody smoked but nobody spoke. The leafless, lifeless Somerset countryside rolled by. Every now and then we'd stop and a few more bleary eyed souls joined us to silently share that Monday morning feeling I would come to know so well.

I can't remember much about my first day at work. A chat with Personnel I imagine and an introduction to everyone in the department, their names sticking in my memory for about as long as it took me to walk to the next desk and be introduced to someone new.

Eventually, 5 o'clock came around. Time to go home. I made my way to the car park and looked for the bus to West Pennard.

It was then that my ordeal began.

The car park was crammed with buses, but which one was mine? As far as I could tell, none were conspicuously or even vaguely West Pennard bound. Their destination boards were ominously blank. How was I to know which bus was going my way? All around me people were happily hopping, skipping and jumping on to their transport home.

How did they know it was the right bus? Was there some sort of secret sign the drivers gave? Was there a nod and a wink that said 'This one's for Bridgwater' or 'This one's for Somerton'? Was there an exchange of glances that translated as 'Weston-Super-Mare? Welcome aboard and enjoy your journey'?

If there was a code, I couldn't crack it.

Too embarrassed to ask for help, I simply stood there, motionless, unlike the buses which, slowly but surely, one by one, were all moving off and leaving the car park.

A horn beeped, mockingly it seemed to me, as the rear lights of the last bus disappeared into the night.

Eventually I was all alone.

There was nothing else for it. I'd have to walk home. To West Pennard. Six miles. In the cold. And dark. I can't recall how long it took, I'm guessing about two hours.

And it was a trek I'd make for at least another 10 days until finally, compelled either by exhaustion or the fear of being mown down by a passing car and left for dead in a ditch, I plucked up the courage to ask which bus went to West Pennard. 'Over there,' said one of the drivers, jerking an oily thumb in the direction of an old green charabanc. Behind the wheel was the fat man in the cap. He gave me a slightly quizzical look as I climbed on board. He was presumably wondering how the hell I'd got home every night for the last two weeks.

In those early days, my self-consciousness knew no bounds.

In my time at Clarks I never once went for lunch in the staff canteen. In my mind, all eyes would be on the new boy as he made his entrance. There would be a hushed silence. Eventually a lone voice would hiss 'You're not from around here are you boy?' I'd try to respond by explaining that actually I was from around here and that actually I was born in....But my words would be drowned out by the sound of cutlery being banged on Formica topped tables. As the cacophony got louder and louder, the clattering beat would be joined by a rhythmic chant of 'Bog Brush! Bog Brush! Bog Brush!'

Crimson with embarrassment, I'd try and run away but within two or three steps be felled by the cold, stainless steel of a carving knife between my retreating shoulder blades. Using a lasso made from a string of sausages, a baying mob would haul my lifeless body back into the canteen.

Then their gnarled and twisted factory worker fingers would start tearing at the still warm flesh of my corpse. They'd stuff great, dripping gobbets of it into their gaping, malevolent maws. They'd gnaw at my bones, fight and pick over the bloody scraps. Like a pack of hungry hell hounds, they would devour every last blushing morsel of me.

Of course that might not happen.

They might just completely ignore me and get on with their lunches and their lives. But I wasn't prepared to take the risk. So instead I wandered around town, eating a cheese roll made by Katina not Katrina.

Sometimes I'd venture into the local cafe. Standing in the queue I'd light up a cigarette, even though I didn't smoke. The idea was to create an actual smokescreen for my awkwardness. But I only ever succeeded in coughing violently, turning a sickly shade of green and drawing even more attention to myself.

Now and then I'd invite myself on to a table to join a couple of lads I knew from the photographic department. I'd nod in agreement at their words of wisdom on the weekend's football results or snigger when they mentioned the size of some girl's tits. I had a thousand witty contributions to add to the banter but never uttered a single one of them. Tomorrow, I thought, I'll slay them with my amusing observations on everything from the 4-2-4 system to the female of the species - *bints* as they preferred to call them.

Tomorrow. Tomorrow. Tomorrow.

CHAPTER 15

POETRY 'N' MOTION

My job at Clarks was Retail Schedule Clerk. These days it would probably be called Local Media Analyst, Strategist, Planner & Buyer.

Basically I drew up - literally, in biro on sheets of A3 paper - local press advertising schedules for Clarks shoe shops the length and breadth of the UK. I'd recommend an 8" double column on this date and an 11" triple column on that date in their local paper. I'd cost it and send the whole lot off to the retailer in question for their approval. If they were happy, they'd send the schedule back, duly signed, and I'd pass it on to Anne and Ray, the dynamic duo who would arrange for the necessary ad blocks to be despatched. Job done.

It was as boring as it sounds. Possibly more boring. I spent hours staring into space. Or at Sue Bonnet, who one day asked if I'd like a photograph. I never dared look at her again.

When I did have something to do, the main tool of my trade was something called British Rate & Data or BRAD for short, a publication which listed all the local papers, from John O'Groats to Lands End, and their ad rates. Also essential to my role was the Dictaphone.

I spent hours on that Dictaphone, dictating letters to accompany my schedules. I can still feel the gently warming press of its Bakelite receiver against my right ear. And every letter I monotonously dictated was exactly the same - only the retailer's name, address and the name of the local paper changed.

It made no sense.

I may have been new to the cut and thrust world of advertising, but within a few weeks even I had worked out that we could create a template and just get the girls in the typing pool to insert the minor changes as required.

My boss, Mervyn, had other ideas.

As precise and immovable in the way he did things as he was in the way he dressed, Mervyn saw no reason to do things differently, particularly at the behest of some 17 year old kid in a cheap Burtons suit.

So the Dictaphone continued to get its daily hammering and every couple of days I would go down to the typing pool and collect my letters, blushing violently and convinced that every girl in its serried rows was sniggering at the way I said 'Yours faithfully, Leon Broome, Retail Schedule Clerk'.

As I say, being a Retail Schedule Clerk was boring. It was also rather sporadic employment.

To fill the time when I wasn't busy scheduling, I was given various other tasks around the department. I sorted out old files and records. I catalogued and collated stuff. And on Fridays I delivered the weekly pay packets, one of my least favourite jobs. People would tear open their little brown envelopes in front of me then berate me for how much tax they'd paid. I tried to explain that I wasn't actually Chancellor of the Exchequer and therefore not responsible for the country's fiscal policy. But my stuttered protestations were usually lost in a tirade of four letter words and abuse, sometimes bordering on the physical.

And, despite the odd jobs I was found to do, I still I had time on my hands.

I occupied myself by writing poetry, often about my fellow workers. It was rarely flattering, but nearly always angry and angsty.

One bile-filled tirade against a colleague began *MH11, Extension 68, eats up the fungus on white canteen plate. Returns to the office all teeth and lips....*

Another started *Hello, Gladys Lockyer, Customer Enquiries. Open your mouths and spew out your diaries.* I can't remember where either of them went after that. To some bitter and twisted conclusion no doubt.

Another I remember in all its brief but spiteful glory. It read, *With his rolled umbrella tucked neatly under his arm, he smiles at the shine on his shoes. But when he leaves this world a dead man, there won't be any clues. No clues that he lived, no clues that he died. Just a thimble full of tears the whole world has cried.*

129

I won't insult the memory of the man I wrote that about by naming him, but needless to say his personality didn't make much of an impression on the shy but strangely superior LMB11, Extension 69.

Over the weeks and months my collected works grew and I actually submitted a selection of poems to a publisher who every year produced an anthology called *New Poets*. It was a vanity publishing deal - they'd chosen five of my poems and wanted £25 to cover costs - but the book was pretty good.

I checked out the previous year's edition at the library. It was a hardback, nicely designed and printed. There was an editorial panel and a proper selection process to help maintain standards. They also guaranteed to distribute the book to libraries, schools and literary journals.

Most importantly, as the publishers explained, it got your work and your name in print and who knew what that might lead to. The £25 fee also included a complimentary copy of the book for each poem published. I was really excited. Work was mind-numbingly dull. I was lonely and missing my friends. I needed a bit of a boost.

Needless to say I didn't have the money - it was more than a month's salary - so I asked good old dad. He wanted to see my poems and judge for himself whether they were worth twenty five quid of his hard-earned cash.

He decided they weren't. And that was that.

My career as a poet was over before it had started. Dad went to his grave not fully comprehending that his act of meanness had denied poetry lovers everywhere access to such classics as *The Reverend Alan Trew-West maintains that sinners be cleansed like drains. Repent and denounce the ways of Old Nick and anoint twice daily with Holy Harpic.*

In the meantime, Christine, my girlfriend, who had gallantly agreed to move to Somerset with me and enroll as a student nurse at Weston-Super-Mare Hospital, was growing increasingly homesick.

Weston was nearby but still too far away for us to see each other except at weekends when she wasn't working. The journey was tortuous too - a country bus that noodled and ambled its way down every imaginable lane and took every detour possible so that 35 miles seemed more like 335.

After a few months she clearly felt more lonely and abandoned than I did (at least I had my sister, Katina not Katrina). She moved back to the Isle of Wight.

Though separated by great swathes of the Somerset, Wiltshire and Hampshire countryside, not to mention the Solent, we still managed to carry on our courtship. I'd ring her whenever I could, which involved a trip to the nearest phone box and a few snatched words before my money ran out. And we wrote to each other. In a grand, romantic gesture I'd pledged to write every day. I think I kept it up but I can't imagine what I found to say - got a new red pen today, did some schedules, had a cheese roll for lunch.

Sometimes I'd add an extra frisson to my *billets doux* by writing SWALK on the back of the envelope. It was short for Sealed With A Loving Kiss. Along with BURMA - Be Undressed And Ready My Angel - and NORWICH - Nickers Off Ready When I Come Home - it was the textese of its day.

As well as phone calls and letters there were weekend visits that involved me hitch-hiking from Street to Portsmouth after work on a Friday.

Looking back, I have no idea how I made that journey, what route I took or what towns and villages I passed through. All I remember is leaving work at 5.00pm, still in my suit, overnight bag in hand. I'd stick my thumb out the minute I hit the pavement outside Clarks' front door and say to anyone who stopped, 'Portsmouth?' I trusted them to know the direction I needed to go, because I certainly didn't. I got better with practice, but even then, sometimes setting off in the dark, I was at the mercy of anyone with even the vaguest idea of where Portsmouth actually was.

By some miracle, bit by bit, car by car and lorry by lorry, a couple of miles here, a few more miles there, I usually made it in time to get the last ferry across to the Island. When I didn't, I was forced to stay in a pub opposite the Portsmouth Guildhall. The Guildhall clock kept me awake all night and so did the thought that bed and breakfast was costing me more than the train fare I'd tried to save by hitching in the first place.

Generally, hitch-hiking was OK in those days. There was the occasional dickhead who'd slow down, stop, then speed off flicking you a V-sign as you were about to jump into the passenger seat, but most of the time people seemed happy to give lifts. There were no thoughts about them murdering you or you murdering them. Most motorists just wanted a bit of company.

The worst thing was gratefully climbing into a car only to discover within minutes that the driver had almost certainly got their license out of a Christmas cracker. Or they were drunk. Or both. You couldn't ask to get out - that would be rude - and besides, a lift was a lift and every mile covered, however erratically, was a mile closer to your destination. So you just had to grin and bear the white-knuckle ride while making polite conversation about what an adventure it was to drive on the wrong side of the road. With no lights. And at 50 miles an hour over the speed limit.

My fantasy was a blonde nymphomaniac in a sports car that ran out of petrol outside a country pub. It would be too late to call the nearest garage and we'd have to stay the night in the pub's only available bedroom - a double of course. One thing would inevitably lead to another.

But it remained a fantasy and I had to make do with long-distance lorry drivers, sales reps and, on one occasion, a soldier who'd driven non-stop from his base in Germany. As the car careered from one side of the A303 to other, he informed me that he'd picked me up in the hope that talking to me would stop him falling asleep at the wheel. Again.

The only other lift I remember in any detail was a bloke in an old Ford Popular. He stopped and said he was only going a couple of miles up the road, but if it helped I was welcome to hop in. Grateful, as ever, for any distance covered I took him up on his offer. A few minutes later we pulled up.

'This is as far as I go,' he said, 'Sorry I can't take you any further'.

What a nice man I thought as I climbed out of the car. 'Thanks anyway,' I said, closing the Popular's passenger door.

I didn't think I'd slammed it, but maybe I did.

Anyway, the passenger door window shattered into a thousand tiny pieces. Shards of glass fell into the car and on to the road. The bloke was speechless. I was speechless. I didn't know what to do.

I knew I couldn't offer to pay for the damage - I was hitch-hiking because I had no money. And I'm guessing the driver had no money either. He looked about my age. And like me, he probably earned a pittance, most of which he probably spent on petrol so he could drive to and from work, stopping on occasions to do a good deed. Like giving some needy soul a lift.

Oh well, I had a ferry to catch.

I walked away briskly, thumb out. I didn't look back. I just hoped and prayed a car would come along and get me out of there as quickly as possible.

A college or university scarf was a very useful prop when it came to getting lifts. Who doesn't want to help a hardworking undergrad get home in time to spend the weekend with their folks?

I had a fake uni scarf - they were quite fashionable at the time - and now and again it did the trick. It was only when I was quizzed about what I was studying, and where, that things got a little awkward. I usually muttered something about a BBC in Applied Geophysnomics at the University of Manchesterwich and hoped for the best.

After about six months at West Pennard, Katina not Katrina, Robert, Danny and I moved into Street - 6, Vestry Road. It was a couple of hundred yards from Clarks, so no more works bus and no more grunted 'Oright' as I made my way to the back. Instead I joined the hordes who walked to work, our pace quickening at the factory hooter's clarion call. The hooter let us know we had just 5 minutes to clock in.

They still made shoes in Street at the time and the office workers were bound by the same time-keeping rules as the men and women on the production line. If you were more than 7 minutes late in the course of a week it was rounded up to quarter of an hour and your pay was docked accordingly. Nobody wanted that. The dent in your savings could have serious repercussions when factory fortnight came around and you needed all the spending money you could muster for your two weeks holiday in a caravan at Westward Ho!

And so it was that the days, weeks and months dragged by.

As my confidence grew around the office I managed to make the days go by a little more quickly by having a joke and a laugh with two or three of the girls in the advertising department. Mervyn, whilst friendly enough, remained as buttoned up as his maroon waistcoat.

Away from work I had no social life. I watched TV most nights with Katina not Katrina and Rob (although the moon landing and A.J.P. Taylor's observation that it was the greatest non-event of his life are about the only two things I remember) or I sat in my bedroom, either strumming doleful, minor chords on my guitar or writing letters to Christine.

I was miserable for the most part and livened up only as the weekend approached and the prospect of a trip to the Isle of Wight got ever closer. By Friday afternoon I was delirious; by Monday morning, down in the dumps again.

It was a cycle that needed to change. And change it did.

CHAPTER 16

THE L IN LONDON

They say everything happens for a reason. And one of the first things that happened to me in 1968, and one of the things that helped me change my life, was the rest of the family moved away. My mum was living with us at Vestry Road at the time - the always precarious relationship with her sister and brother-in-law had tipped over into irreconcilable differences and mum had moved out. Suddenly Katina not Katrina announced they were all off to Eastbourne. It probably wasn't as brutal as that, but the long and the short of it was I needed somewhere else to live.

The fabulously named Marlene Haddock came to the rescue.

I worked alongside her, she was fun and we got on well and when I confided in Marlene about my predicament she said no problem, her parents took in lodgers and they had a room available right now. It was a few doors along on Vestry Road and it was going cheap because Marlene had to walk through my room to get to hers. The rent included breakfast, lunch, an evening meal and a late night supper of sandwiches, digestive biscuits and a hot, milky drink.

So, a couple of weeks later, after I'd waved goodbye to Katina not Katrina, Robert, Danny and mum (and Boo Boo), I moved into my new digs, warmly welcomed by the Haddocks - Marlene, her mum, her dad and David, her monosyllabic brother. But no matter how hard they tried to make me feel at home, I still wasn't convinced this was the new dawn I was looking for.

So, as well as writing letters to Christine, who was making plans to resume her nurse's training in London, I started writing letters to advertising agencies, also in London. I got names and addresses out of a guide we had at work and set myself an initial target of 50 agencies. I wanted a job, any job, that would help me get a foot in the door and from there take that first step to realising my ultimate goal of becoming a copywriter.

From J. Walter Thompson to Benton & Bowles, from Foote Cone & Belding to Bates, they all got my missives seeking any kind of gainful employment. And they all responded in exactly the same way - *Dear Leon, Thank you for your letter and we appreciate your interest in (insert agency name as appropriate) but we regret to inform you that....* You can guess the rest.

With depressing regularity, these *We regret to inform yous* dropped on to the Haddocks' doormat, each one another nail in the coffin of my hopes and dreams. Then, as I neared my target of 50 letters, I got a reply that offered a glimmer of hope.

An agency in Knightsbridge called Golley Slater couldn't offer me a job but they could offer me some of their time - an account executive called Tony would happily spare me an hour or so to chat about how I might eventually break into advertising.

It was better than nothing and as soon as I could I high-tailed it up to London for the day. Tony was friendly, the chat was useful and not entirely discouraging, but still no job at the end of it.

As I left Golley Slater, uncertain of how I felt about my chances of ever finding work with a London ad agency, I noticed a branch of Alfred Marks, the employment bureau, on the opposite side of the road

I thought about it for a moment then decided I had nothing to lose by popping in and asking if they could get me a job in advertising. I began telling the man from Alfred Marks all about life as a Retail Schedule Clerk and before I'd even got to the really exciting bit about Ray and Ann sending off the ad blocks, he was on the phone to Lintas, an agency name that rang a bell thanks to my hit list of 50.

Lintas were looking for something called an Assistant TV Time Buyer. I had an interview that afternoon and a job by the end of the week. It was that easy. If only I'd known before I wasted all that Quink ink, all that Basildon Bond and all those threepenny stamps.

Ironically, while I was working my week's notice at Clarks I got a job offer from Golley Slater. I felt really bad because they'd been so kind, but I had to turn them down. I wrote back saying *Dear Tony, Thank you for your letter and I appreciate your interest in me but I regret to inform you that....* You can guess the rest.

On my last day at Clarks there was a short speech from Mike Phelps, who ran the department, and I was given a card and a leaving present. The present was about the size of a tea chest and wrapped in brown paper tied up with string. I stood there in front of everyone, mumbling something about missing them all (in truth I was only going to miss Marlene, Jean and Geraldine) and all the while I was wrestling with acres of paper and miles of string. Before I got to the Parker pen and pencil set that was concealed deep, deep, deep inside the comically oversized package, I'd given myself quite a bad and rather painful paper cut. My face was about as red as my spilled blood by the time the whole sorry spectacle came to an end.

So, I was off to London.

I knew how I was going to get there. I'd suggested to Jean that her boyfriend might like to take her up to see the bright lights of the big city. She thought that sounded like a lovely idea. 'And if you are going,' I said, as if butter wouldn't melt in my mouth, 'Perhaps you could make it this Friday and give me a lift'.

It was a slightly sneaky thing to do, but I got my free ride and Jean got her romantic evening, strolling along the South Bank arm in arm with her Brian. They dropped me off on Waterloo Bridge. It was a short walk back to Waterloo train station where I deposited all my stuff - basically a suitcase and a guitar - in left luggage.

Now I needed somewhere to stay. Christine was already in London. She'd started her nurse's training again and was living in a student nurses' home on Euston Road.

But I couldn't stay with her. Just visiting her room, let alone staying overnight, was absolutely forbidden by hospital rules and would have got her into serious trouble with Matron. Which is why, when I'd been up to London a couple of times to visit, I'd ended up staying in a flea-bitten hotel just down the road in Kings Cross.

Unlike now, Kings Cross then was bit of a dive and I was convinced that a lot of the hotels were also brothels. I was also convinced any woman who looked at me was a prostitute. God knows how many perfectly innocent secretaries, wending their way home after a hard day at the office, were confused by a skinny, ginger-haired youth in a shiny Burtons suit vigorously shaking his head and politely but firmly saying 'No thank you'.

Anyway, I couldn't think of anywhere else to go.

So Kings Cross it was where, for about £7 a week, I got bed, breakfast and the distinct feeling that I might contract any number of sexually transmitted diseases from the bed linen.

It was November 1969 and that night, as I cautiously laid my head on the pillow and listened to the rumble of the city, the sirens and the raised, drunken voices outside my bedroom window, I wondered what next?

ABOUT THE AUTHOR

When he was 10 years old Leon Broome had a story read out on BBC radio. He missed it. He'd gone out to play. A couple of years later he was sending hand-written lyrics to the music publishers along London's Tin Pan Alley. From Northern Songs to Dick James Music, they all failed to spot the potential in his unique, if slightly immature, way with words about love, life and two big giants who were having some fun.

In his 20s he co-wrote the songs and played guitar for *Waiter My Bill*, a band the late John Peel name-checked but sadly never got to see before they split up unable, on occasions, to carry a tune in a bucket.

In his 30s he was briefly one half of *What the Blazes!*, a duo whose comedy was described as 'distinctive' by The Stage newspaper but whose ambitions went up in haze of cigarette smoke and alcohol fumes accompanied by a barrage of abuse late one night at Soho's Comedy Store. He had a short story, *The Man Who Came to Christmas Dinner*, published in Marxism Today (nothing to do with politics, plenty to do with wanting to see his name in print) and he appeared in the back room of a West London pub as the Earth Spirit in a fringe theatre production of

Goethe's *Faust*. Favourably reviewed by the Guardian, it didn't transfer to the West End.

In his 40s he had some one liners rejected by comedians Hale and Pace and a sitcom, *Not Fade Away,* on option with a producer who also commissioned him to turn *A Midsummer Night's Dream* into a musical (Leon's dreams of success with either never came true, but that's another story). He also had a three minute radio play - *Inside Information* starring Lorcan Cranitch and Bryan Murray - broadcast on Classic fm.

More recently, he has declaimed some of his poetry to an indifferent audience at the Salisbury Arts Centre, while *Needs Must*, his cautionary tale of what happens when the devil drives, appeared on a short story website to critical acclaim…well, one reader (quite possibly his wife) said 'Ace! 5 Star!'

In 2015, he was shortlisted for the Winston Fletcher Fiction Prize. He didn't take home first prize but took some consolation from the fact that the winner was a published author with several books to his *nom de plume*.

He has a screenplay for a feature length film somewhere on his laptop.

He's managed bands, worked in cafes and bars and owned a health food shop and herb store. He's been a local press planner/ buyer, an assistant TV time buyer, a progress controller and an account exec. He's been a warehouseman, a market research gopher and the guy who checks the answers on multiple choice exam papers. He was a petrol pump attendant for an afternoon and sold (or rather didn't sell) double glazing for a week. He's auditioned at RADA and applied for teacher training college. But mostly he's been an advertising copywriter.

Married for the first time before he was 20, he was married for the third time before he was 40.

He's a trier.

And now he's trying to tell his story in this frank and often very funny book about his early years.

ACKNOWLEDGEMENTS

Thanks to Johnny Bull for the front cover, Joe Broome for his technical support, Chris Howe for his prowess with punctuation, Mandy Wheeler for her words of encouragement, and all my friends and family for the memories.

Printed in Great Britain
by Amazon